Praise for *I Don't Do Disability and
Other Lies I've Told Myself*

At its heart, *I Don't Do Disability and Other Lies I've Told Myself*
is a story about creativity and love, the essential ingredients necessary to harness the wildness and the wonder of our world, and, in
Purdham's case, to face down inherent ableism, both in herself and
others. Purdham shows us that disability is life, and she illustrates
this with fierce veracity and through intensely readable prose, writing with a wisdom and clarity that comes from great self-reflection
and research, but also via the simple act of living. The final scene is
astonishing in its beauty and clear-eyed revelation. I clipped it from
the manuscript and hung it on my office wall.

— EMILY URQUHART, author of *Ordinary Wonder Tales*

A marvel of tenderness and ferocity. The voice of these essays is that
of a devoted parent, a tireless advocate, and a generous thinker.
Every line is shaped by Purdham's powerful sense of integrity: her
insistence on seeing things for exactly what they are and her willingness to imagine what they might one day become.

— MANDY LEN CATRON, author of
How to Fall in Love with Anyone

Searching, intimate, and above all, honest, these essays about
friendship, marriage, parenting, disability, and the risks and joys of
a writing life reverberate, nourish, challenge, and shine. If it's true
that the way we do anything is the way we do everything, Adelle
Purdham does everything with frankness and fierce love.

— SUSAN OLDING, author of *Big Reader*

The disability community deplores books by disability-adjacent writers where parents, spouses, and siblings of disabled people make fame and fortune centring themselves as disabled saviours. This is not that book. Refreshingly and importantly, Adelle Purdham has instead centred her struggle with her own ableism. An unflinching examination from girlhood to marriage to motherhood, she peels back the layers of society's ableist onion to reveal and reject the negative attitudes that limited her thinking. To be the mother her disabled daughter deserves, she accepts the challenge to "do disability," becoming a parent disability advocate. A welcome addition to disability literature in Canada.

— DOROTHY ELLEN PALMER, disability activist
and author of *Falling for Myself*

In essays both raw and daring, Adelle Purdham takes a hard look at what it is to be a wife and mother deeply in love with her family and the life she's made with them, without losing herself in the melee. From a fractious walk home from school with her children to a late-night skinny dip with a friend, these essays are about moments that transcend the everyday and give us, one glimpse at a time, a sense of a larger whole.

— JANE SILCOTT, author of *Everything Rustles*

I Don't Do Disability and Other Lies I've Told Myself is a staggering examination of privilege and ableism and of the intimate and often painful complexities and hypocrisies of self. By mining the depths of her own prejudices and biases, Purdham encourages us to do the same. This book breathes resolve and tenderness. It is a profound testament to how our children teach us more than we'll ever teach them. A must-read.

— HOLLAY GHADERY, author of *Fuse*

We ask of memoirists the impossible: tell us everything, as if we are the best of friends sitting at your kitchen table; reveal the best of you, and the worst, too. Make it so compelling, I can't put it down. And most of all: don't hold anything back. Adelle Purdham's *I Don't Do Disability and Other Lies I've Told Myself* delivers in this must-read memoir, on all counts. She welcomes the reader as companion, not voyeur, and then she spills it all: the love and joy and rage and uncertainty and everything in between. And don't let the title trick you into thinking this is a book with a single theme — Purdham tackles not just her own internalized ableism after the birth of her daughter with Down syndrome, but also modern marriage, parenting in general, the pull of a creative life, desire, womanhood, the solace of nature, the urgency of advocacy in our modern world, and so much more. Purdham's fearless honesty and vulnerability fill these pages with magic. This is a stunning debut.

— CHRISTINA MYERS, author of *Halfway Home*

An extraordinary memoir that takes us on an arduous journey of heartbreak and evolving new ways of perceiving love — even meaning itself.

— BETSY WARLAND, author of *Breathing the Page*

With earnest candour and a whole lot of heart, Adelle Purdham puts the essayistic form to its best use: to think through the vagaries of human experience and question fixed beliefs, whether our own or the received wisdom of the culture in which we swim. I loved riding shotgun with Purdham's kind, funny, and unflinchingly sharp observations. This book is a vehicle of expansion.

— COOPER LEE BOMBARDIER, author of *Pass with Care*

A tender, beautifully written essay collection that is about so much more than parenting a child with a disability. Purdham delivers vivid, introspective prose that reveals a keen intellect and strong sense of self-awareness on every page. As she navigates everything from systemic challenges and personal overwhelm to uncovering her own biases, Purdham writes with illuminating candour. This is a book about a loving, devoted mother who is not a saint, nor should she be.

— ERIN PEPLER, author of *Send Me Into the Woods Alone*

I DON'T DO DISABILITY

And Other Lies I've Told Myself

I DON'T DO DISABILITY

And Other Lies I've Told Myself

ADELLE PURDHAM

DUNDURN
PRESS

This book is a memoir that reflects the author's present recollections of experiences over time. Some names and characteristics have been changed, some events have been compressed, and some dialogue has been recreated.

Excerpts from "A Country of Marriage," copyright © 1971, 1972, 1973 by Wendell Berry, from *A Country of Marriage*. Reprinted by permission of Counterpoint Press.

Excerpt from "Pole Star," copyright © 2019 by Kim Fehner, from *These Wings*. Reprinted by permission of Kim Fehner.

Publisher: Meghan Macdonald | Acquiring editor: Megan Beadle
Cover designer: Laura Boyle
Cover image: horse: istock/visiostyle; fir: istock/Sylfida; oak leaf: istock/Olga Shalimova; loon: shutterstock/Michel Legault

Library and Archives Canada Cataloguing in Publication

Title: I don't do disability and other lies I've told myself / Adelle Purdham.
Other titles: I do not do disability and other lies I've told myself
Names: Purdham, Adelle, author.
Description: Includes bibliographical references.
Identifiers: Canadiana (print) 20240364546 | Canadiana (ebook) 20240364562 | ISBN 9781459754539 (softcover) | ISBN 9781459754546 (PDF) | ISBN 9781459754553 (EPUB)
Subjects: LCSH: Purdham, Adelle. | LCSH: Mothers of children with Down syndrome—Canada— Biography. | LCGFT: Autobiographies.
Classification: LCC RJ506.D68 P87 2024 | DDC 618.92/8588420092—dc23

We acknowledge the support of the Canada Council for the Arts and the Ontario Arts Council for our publishing program. We also acknowledge the financial support of the Government of Ontario, through the Ontario Book Publishing Tax Credit and Ontario Creates, and the Government of Canada.

Care has been taken to trace the ownership of copyright material used in this book. The author and the publisher welcome any information enabling them to rectify any references or credits in subsequent editions.

The publisher is not responsible for websites or their content unless they are owned by the publisher.

Dundurn Press
1382 Queen Street East
Toronto, Ontario, Canada M4L 1C9
dundurn.com, @dundurnpress

For Elyse,
Dan, Ariel, and Penelope

Contents

Nature

MOTHER

Three, Two, One

"WHAT DO YOU want me to write?" I ask the editor.

"*What is it you need to say?*" the editor says without saying it.

Essay. *J'essai.* I try to form the words.

Maybe if I snap my fingers, this piece will write itself, easy as *one, two, three.*

One

It's 2:00 a.m. and I wake with the sensation of having to pee. Our bed, with its deluxe pillowtop, is plush and high, thanks to my dad's career as a mattress salesman. At thirty-eight weeks pregnant, I had experienced mild contractions earlier in the day, when my husband, Dan, and I picked up the groceries and walked our friends' dog, but by evening — silence. As I slide my legs out of bed to the floor, there's a distinct pop, followed by the telltale gush of warm fluid.

I wake Dan up, and the minutes tick by as labour progresses and the pain increases with each contraction tearing through my body. I pace the hardwood floors of our living room, then stand with both hands on the back of our brown faux-leather couch and think, *I don't want to do this anymore.*

Too late.

The pain amps up to a ten on the suffer scale; meanwhile, quickly, efficiently, my body is willing this baby out. On the fifteen-minute ride to the hospital, my bottom never touches the seat. I writhe through the contractions, wild-eyed, as Dan grips the steering wheel tightly with both hands.

I arrive at the hospital ten centimetres dilated. No time for pain relief; no need for medical intervention. I push for half an hour, and then at 4:36 a.m. — two hours after I slid out of bed and my water broke — our eldest daughter is born. We name her Ariel Marie in tribute to my matriarchal lineage, my Grandma Marie who gave me my love for tea and the garden's bounty. Ariel latches beautifully and takes to breastfeeding right away. A five out of five Apgar score; her heart rate is steady, muscle tone and reflexes strong, overall health good. Textbook, perfect.

We leave the hospital, babe in arms, by 4:30 p.m. the same day.

This part of the story is easy to write. In society's eyes, a twenty-seven-year-old woman giving birth feels right, normal.

✳

I should listen to my editor. "*We generally tend toward personal narrative that avoids editorializing too much.*"

✳

Two

Nine-month-old Ariel blows raspberries onto the mirror of our bedroom closet. Around this age, babies begin to establish their sense of self as separate from their caregivers, and Ariel's delighted to have found her person on the other side of the glass.

A few months earlier, Dan and I talked about having a second child, a sibling for Ariel. We wanted to wait until she was a year old before we tried again, to give ourselves a chance to catch our breath. In the meantime, my birth control pills ran out.

To a symphony of squashing sounds and farting noises made with baby saliva, I hold up the pregnancy test. The faint line means only one thing — *positive.*

Dan arrives home with flowers and a card that reads "Special Delivery" and "It's a Girl!" "It's a Girl" is an inside joke between us, something about Dan always knowing he'd be surrounded by women; "Special Delivery" is a prescient misnomer.

＊

"Allow the story to do the heavy lifting," the editor tells me.

Yes, I'd prefer it that way.

＊

After my twenty-week ultrasound, there's a message from the midwife on our home phone.

Dan listens to the message. "She says to call her?"

There's a question in his voice.

That's odd, I think. *There was never any follow-up after my twenty-week ultrasound with Ariel.*

I lean onto our brown faux-leather couch with one knee and look out our large bay window at the trees thrashing in the wind, their leaves catching light from the sun. I tuck my newly cropped hair behind my ear, a sure sign of my mother-ness, and call the midwife back.

"The results from your twenty-week ultrasound are in," she says slowly, choosing her words, "and they show a soft marker for Down syndrome."

Down syndrome?

I say the words out loud. Dan's eyes burn on the back of my neck from across the room, where he's building a block tower with Ariel.

The tower comes down with a crash. Ariel squeals with delight.

✺

"We're interested in precision," the editor says. *"The selection of just the right word that saves the writer the need to add another sentence."*

✺

Before the certainty of a diagnosis, instead of being paralyzed with fear of the unknown, I blocked the questions from my mind. I spent those days of waiting caring for Ariel, who was barely fifteen months old. Our lives continued with a semblance of normalcy — what choice did I have? I would pack books and a picnic of snacks in her ladybug backpack, and we would read together under the shade of the large black walnut tree that covered a section of our backyard. The sun shone magnificently overhead, its rays poking delicately through the leaves. There were the sharp blades of grass, and the smell of freshly cut lawns. Ariel's glowing, soft wisps of hair. Our lives had been crisp and clear. Ariel sat neatly enfolded in my lap, focused and peaceful, carefully letting the pages of her book unfold, and I thought, blinking back the tears, *will it be like this again?*

Two weeks later, after a blood test and a repeat ultrasound, we know for certain. I find the leather couch, curl onto my side and pull my knees in as tight as my pregnant belly will allow, and wail. I cry because I never wanted a baby with Down syndrome. I cry over this new identity being foisted on me as a mother. I cry for hours, and then cry at my crying in the first place. *What will people think?*

I invite Dan into my grieving, and we are two mounds of wet clay, one pile of mush trying to hold the other pile of mush together, to no avail. I push him away and slam my fists into the cushions and then the pillows of our bed, then cry myself into an exhausted sleep.

"We tend to shy away from stories that are overly sentimental," says the editor.

When a baby is born with Down syndrome, their placenta also has Down syndrome. Down syndrome is not a medical condition on its own, but it is associated with a host of medical concerns, the most prevalent and immediate worry involving the heart. The second most common concern is gastrointestinal issues.[1]

When I am thirty-six weeks and five days pregnant, our baby's placenta stops functioning properly and the time arrives for her to come out.

Dan and I were right about the girl, just wrong about everything else.

We enter the hospital, Tim Hortons cups in hand, feeling quite relaxed. The medical staff informs me I will be induced lying down so they can monitor the baby's heartbeat. I managed the pain in my first pregnancy with movement — pacing the room, swaying, bracing myself against the leather couch. I ask for an epidural.

On her first attempt, the young anesthesiologist pushes the needle too far, puncturing the dura mater and arriving at my spinal fluid.

She walks around to face me.

"I'm so sorry," she says, "you're going to get the worst headache of your life whenever you sit up for the next few weeks. And I'm going to have to do it again."

"Okay," I say, because what else do you say to the person holding the large needle that's about to re-pierce your spine?

I never did get that headache. Not everything is as bad as it seems.

With the steady drip of Pitocin, labour progresses. Dan and I listen to music, and we're laughing together over something I can no longer remember when the nurse arrives.

"Look at those rosy cheeks," she says. "Your body is working hard."

I can't feel a thing. I think that is the joke.

After fifteen minutes of pushing and some mild discomfort, the baby arrives, all four pounds, six ounces of her. We name her Elyse, the name of a character from a movie Dan and I watched together, like this isn't real life. She is whisked away for suctioning and scrutiny under bright lights. I don't think about what I'm not doing: holding her, breastfeeding, oohing over how cute she is. Instead, I float somewhere in the room, over my body, watching the scene as they take Elyse away to prep her for the inevitable surgery. She will have abdominal surgery for a blockage in her small intestine the next day. We knew this was coming — but that doesn't ease the heartache.

When your baby has Down syndrome, you are followed at a high-risk clinic and the pregnancy is monitored closely. Our baby has duodenal atresia: "atresia," meaning a blockage, in the "duodenum," the first section of the small intestine. In my pregnancy, the doctor drew a snake in the form of a whoopee cushion with a sharp line blocking the opening to illustrate.

Breastfeeding would have to wait.

※

Down syndrome is characterized by a tripling of the twenty-first chromosome. World Down Syndrome Day, sanctioned by the United Nations in 2012,[2] is celebrated on March 21 (3/21). *Three, two, one.*

※

"We're interested in making sure that what the writer wants to say is actually on the page: it is specific, sharp," explains the editor.

※

Three

Three years have passed since the birth of my second child. I'm thirty years old. We move houses, and the faux-leather couch makes its way to the curb. The tingling in my breasts tells me with certainty that I am indeed pregnant for a third time, after two months of trying. Pregnancy comes easy to me. Motherhood is hard.

She's late. I'm past forty weeks and as summer presses in, I'm ready to meet this baby. I decide on a home birth. An inflatable water tub, which Dan will fill when the time comes, takes up space in our bathroom.

My labour begins after a trip to the midwife clinic and a gentle exam. Even though I've been through labour before, this time feels different; every time feels different. My husband prepares a special dinner for us, spaghetti squash burrito bowls, the colour of the bright purple cabbage and red peppers popping against the yellow squash. The children eat something benign, like chicken nuggets.

As Dan sits down to eat, I pace the room.

"Fill the tub," I inform him, calmly but assertively.

The water in the birthing tub barely reaches my ankles by the time I'm bearing down on all fours on top of our bed.

"Call the midwife — get the kids in bed!" I'm calling out orders.

Dan, not wanting to leave me, runs back and forth like the proverbial chicken with its head cut off.

"Fuck!" I swear with the pain of her head cresting, but I do want to do this; I've done it twice before. I choose this pain, and I want this baby out of me.

Our third daughter's head emerges at the exact moment our midwife's hands arrive to safely guide her into the world. Penelope's physical body weighs just over seven pounds.

In my heart, all three of my babies weigh the same.

*

"I'm glad you had that nice birth," a midwife tells me later, "after your last experience."

I know what she means to say. She means to say that the last birth was hard on me, emotionally. After her surgery, Elyse was in the hospital for four and a half weeks. The midwife means to say, *it's a relief this birth was easier than the last.* But there's a subtext to her statement that pulls me under, into the dark deep. The idea that some birth experiences are not nice or desirable, and therefore *less;* like somehow my birth experience with Elyse was unworthy.

Like she expects that, as the mother, I am trying again to get things right. Like, by having another child, my husband and I are striving to erase the past instead of adding more love to our family. I reject what she's assuming about me, about my daughter with Down syndrome, about the value of a life. I know what she means to say. But what I also hear is what's not being said: *I'm glad you had that nice birth, after giving birth to a child with Down syndrome.*

✼

Final note from the editor: *"Subject matter is less important than execution or form. Craft is of the utmost importance."*

When it comes to my daughter, I have learned that craft is not of the utmost importance. Love is.

✼

When I hold Elyse in my arms for the first time, my heart swells and sways. Ten tiny fingers, mouth in the shape of an *oh*. Her small, diapered bottom rests in the palm of my hand as I inhale her milky scent, stroke her downy skin. She is everything a baby should be.

Eleven Years a Country

POETRY SEGMENTS FROM "The Country of Marriage" by Wendell Berry:[1]

I.
I dream of you walking at night along the streams
of the country of my birth[2]

Pre-marriage

We meet walking our dogs, university students colliding into each other like two strangers in a foreign land. Our pathways are a figure eight, the shape of infinity. Again, and again, our routes cross, four times, until finally we come face to face on the sidewalk and you tell me your name, which I forget, but you use mine with a softness that catches my attention when asking whether I'll walk dogs with you. How could I not say yes?

We meet and walk, and we are like tourists in the land of one another, searching for a common language. We invent our own names for things. "Our park" refers to the place behind the house you share with your roommates; the "warm spot" inside my apartment building is the glass enclosure where we meet — oh, how you laughed when I called it that. We rename our dogs, from failed past relationships, after their neighbourhood look-alikes. Oreo, my black-and-white Shih Tzu, becomes Sasha, the Shih Tzu on my apartment floor, and Sumo, your black Lab, becomes Shadow, another Lab on the street, whenever we forget doggie-poo bags.

"Bad boy, Sasha!"

Naming becomes our common ground; it's also a way of laying claim to something.

You are single. I have a boyfriend. I didn't tell you that part, did I? Not at first.

Later, you confess to having a nickname for me. Your roommates know me as "the dog-walking babe."

"Yeah right, Purdham," they say. "I bet you made her up."

I am flattered, cheeks rosy on those cold walks.

Here, at the beginning, we are an imaginary place. What we have is undefined.

II.
And then there rose in me,
like the earth's empowering brew rising
in root and branch, the words of a dream of you
I did not know I had dreamed. I was a wanderer
who feels the solace of his native land
under his feet again and moving in his blood.

The temperature drops to thirty below, and there you are, walking over to meet me with your big black dog, hot chocolate in hand. We conspire to meet again later, in the warm spot. I taste the gooey sweetness of marshmallows and liquid cocoa, and it burns my tongue. I watch the steam from my cup rise and rise in wonder.

III.
Sometimes our life reminds me
of a forest in which there is a graceful clearing
and in that opening a house,
an orchard and garden,
comfortable shades, and flowers
red and yellow in the sun, a pattern
made in the light for the light to return to.

On one of our dog walks, I tell you the truth, that I have a boyfriend, even though he won't last. You stop walking, mid-step, and give me a hurt look — eyes wide, chin dropped loose. You say nothing.

Later, at the movies with my boyfriend — our final date — I receive a text from you:

> *I was really disappointed to hear that today. I'll still walk dogs with you.*

III.
The forest is mostly dark, its ways
to be made anew day after day, the dark
richer than the light and more blessed,
provided we stay brave
enough to keep on going in.

Year 11

We fight. We fight about parenting, about responsibilities — about *who* exactly is responsible for what. Is the emotional labour I provide invisible to you? I feel like the tree that falls in the forest — do I make a sound? I tell you that you suck. At the pinnacle of my rage,

I hurl insults at you, call you by unspeakable names. I am not so easily tamed; I am the wild beast of this country, both praised for what I have to offer and caged in gender roles that silence.

We are in the dark thick of the forest. I speak on behalf of oppressed women, while understanding I belong to the most privileged among them. "I spent ten years of my life fully devoted to raising our kids. And I chose to do that, we chose to live our lives that way, but things *change*. And I know you've made sacrifices too — but I didn't promise to stay home forever. And now it's *my turn*." I speak from a place of frustration and outrage. "Nobody would ever question why you would need babysitting to do your job!"

When a woman wants to work, she is selfish, abandoning her children. I break the silence. *My mind is not worth the same as your mind because I have used my hands to raise children, while yours have raised dollars.* A woman is free only if she's free to do as she pleases without guilt.

I speak my truth: "I need space and time to work without being made to feel bad about it; I need you to be in charge of the kids." You speak yours, "Change is hard." You listen, I shout. You are not the oppressor, I know, but you benefit from the ways I am oppressed.

> IV.
> I come to you
> lost, wholly trusting as a man who goes
> into the forest unarmed.

We drive down a private road, no children with us, our new puppy crated in the back. We plan to take him on a hike in this new place we've arrived at. We own a cottage, not far from here. We stand together at the base of the hill, deciding whether to go up or not. We might get lost, you worry.

"Come on!" I say, starting up the rugged path. "Let's just see where this goes," and you follow. When we reach the top, we look down on cascading hills of lush forest with a wide, sparkling river carved through the middle. From here, the sun's light touches everything; only the clouds create pockets of shadows. We climbed to get here and now we admire this wild country, its luminous trees glowing gold before us.

V.
We are more together
than we know

Year 4

We sit, knees pressed together in the waiting room. My belly is as full as the moon. The fetus inside, our second daughter, has just been diagnosed with Down syndrome.

"Twenty-four weeks is the latest you can legally have an abortion in Canada," the obstetrician tells us. "So if you wanted to get one …"

I worry, for a split second that feels like eternity, that you might have changed your mind.

We had this conversation, years ago, on one of our early dog walks.

"What about if I got pregnant and the baby has special needs?" I asked then.

"Well, it would be our child, right?" you said.

We both agreed.

"No," you cut the obstetrician off. "We don't want that."

I exhale my relief.

V.
and you are the known place to which the
unknown is always
leading me back.

Pre-marriage

It's the week before our wedding and I get a call at work. This unusual page to the office is enough to make my pulse quicken.

"I got in a car accident," you say over the phone.

"What? Are you okay? Is everyone okay? What happened?"

"I rear-ended the lady in front of me. I'm okay. Everyone's okay."

"What about the car?"

The car has been sold and is being picked up the next day. The. Next. Day. The money from the car sale is to pay for our honeymoon.

"Smashed."

We are both shaken up. Permission is granted for me to leave my class of six-year-olds and go home to you, my fiancé. *What if something worse had happened to you?* I can't shake my uneasiness. We take our dogs for a walk to calm down, to return to safety and what is known. Our fingers intertwined, the warmth of our palms touching, the shiver of excitement I still experience in your company, form the stable ground we stand on. When our hands fall apart, we lean close to one another, heads tilted, shoulders touching so that the fabric of our jacket sleeves catches with a swish swish.

We don't see the dog coming that sets off our dogs and sends you careening out of the way and into the cedar branch.

"I cut my head." You show me your hand, which touched your scalp. Blood stains your fingers.

At the emergency room, you get ten staples to hold together the torn skin. I forbid you from doing anything else the rest of the day.

> VI.
> we keep returning
> to its rich waters thirsty.

We are at a friend's wedding. We are sitting at a large, round table, half with friends, half with strangers. I've had a few drinks, quite a few drinks, and my jaw is loose, my view hazy. I'm drawn to the man seated across from me and can't figure out why, until I finally put my finger on it. He notices me noticing him.

"Hey," I tell him, "you look like my ex-boyfriend."

The man sizes me up. "He must have been a good-looking guy, then."

And in that moment, I realize we are flirting, and that I want the flirting, and that I want more than that. I want this man to pull me onto the dance floor. I'm less interested in spending the evening with you, and a familiar shame pulls at my insides, but I ignore it.

It's not like we're married.

The next morning, I'm hungover and tearful as you drive us home. Nothing happened. Everything happened.

"What's wrong?" you ask.

"Nothing — well, you know that guy sitting across the table from us? It's just … I was attracted to him."

I'm crying now; big, warm tears trail down my face.

"Yeah — so what?" you say.

"No, you don't understand. I wanted to do something about it."

"But you didn't."

"But I did before." Not to you, but still.

"But you didn't this time, and you wouldn't have."

You are adamant, and it is then I realize you know me better than I know myself, and that I trust you. I trust you, fully, the way you trust me.

VII.
I give you the life I have let live for the love of
    you:
a clump of orange-blooming weeds beside the
    road,
the young orchard waiting in the snow, our own
    life
that we have planted in the ground, as I
have planted mine in you.

The night before our wedding, we rehearse, facing each other beside the water, holding hands. Just before the rehearsal — the heat too oppressive, the urge so great I can take it no longer — I jump into the lake. And so I stand before you, wholly myself, dripping wet and without a towel, in my white sundress with the thin straps and the oversized purple flowers. And you take me as I am.

Beside a glittering lake, we say our vows. We plant the seed of our marriage and sow a country to call our own.

A fierce gust drowns out the ceremony. We are encircled by our own vortex of wind where sound carries only as far as the other, and so we pronounce the words to one another. To onlookers, we mouth our own private anthem.

The Golden Hour

The sun is a flower that blooms for just one hour.[1]
— Ray Bradbury, "All Summer in a Day"

IN ELEMENTARY SCHOOL, I watch the film version of Ray Bradbury's short story "All Summer in a Day." We are several classes gathered into the library, huddled around one of the shared television and VCR sets. We sit with our legs crossed, hands neatly in our laps, necks craned up toward the artificial blue light. Our faces take on an eerie glow from the lit screen.

In one of the scenes, a young girl is locked in a room. Her knees are pulled into her chest and she's sobbing. This is the saddest thing I have ever seen. The sun was taken from her.

⁕

I nursed Elyse as an infant and into toddlerhood, sitting in the rocking chair in her nursery. A patch of sunlight filtered through the blinds and landed on my arm. The beams of light held dancing motes of dust suspended mid-air. Cradled in my arms, nestled against my flesh, Elyse often submitted to sleep. A tower of children's board books stood beside us on the dark IKEA nightstand, as well as a circus-themed music box that operated with a crank, a gift from Elyse's grandparents. The music box played the tune "Für Elise," composed by Beethoven, who himself was disabled. For Elyse. Elyse's song.

Bradbury's story is set on Venus in a dystopian future where the sun emerges once every seven years, and for only one golden hour. We follow a group of school children who are forever trapped indoors, who spend time daily under sun lamps. The skies are perpetually grey and rainy. Most of the children have never seen the sun and of those who have, none of them remember what it's like, with the exception of one new student, Margot. Margot arrived from Earth only five years earlier and the other children are jealous of her. Only Margot remembers the sensation of the sun. Collectively, the children count down the weeks, days, hours until the sun's appearance, but it is Margot who is most excited. Moments before the sun's arrival, the teacher steps out. A bully tricks Margot into believing the sun isn't coming, and in that created confusion, he and the other children push Margot into a utility closet and lock the door. A moment later, the sky lightens, the teacher returns to summon her students, who run outside in ecstasy, and they forget Margot completely. Margot's muffled screams and bangs on the locked door go unheard. She is abandoned, left behind.

Day after day, Elyse in my lap, I played her tune. I guided her fingers to the crank and helped her turn the dial, but her fingers would alight, splay outward, as though the handle were hot to the touch. Grasping was beyond her skill set. I wanted badly for her to use the music box the way it was meant to be used. Her chubby hands pushed the toy up into her face, and she brought the crank to her mouth. The only sound was the clang of the music box dropping to the floor. I wanted desperately to hear her song, the way it should be played.

I cradled Elyse in my arms. Playtime and storytime had ended. The sun descended in one fell swoop into the earth. The slack weight of Elyse's being pressed against my breast. With one deft finger, I broke her latch; one tear of milk ran from the corner of her wet mouth. I transported her limp body to the soft cotton mattress of her crib, laid a blanket over her torso. Her hands were cupped by her face like half moons, wispy hair curled around the backs of her ears. I smoothed two fingers along the creases of her forehead. The motion soothed her. Then I bent over the crib railing to kiss her plump cheek, careful not to wake her.

She remained a baby much longer than most babies, which I both appreciated and loathed. The contradictory feelings were like nostalgia for a past that never was, hope for a future that would not be.

*

In the original short story "All Summer in a Day," as readers we are with the narrator and the school children outside, witnessing their jubilation at the sun's return, the rapid growth of the flowers, the planet awakening. We don't experience Margot's perspective. But in the film version, we see Margot sitting on the floor, scrunching her knees into her chest, sobbing, holding herself. A crack in the door filters in a shaft of light that eventually fades away, and we know, as Margot does, that she has missed the sun. The sun was taken from her.

I will never forget viewing this scene as a child, the shaft of sunlight withdrawing and the sense of injustice burning in my chest. I felt that child's agony as viscerally as if it were my own. That scene represented two of the saddest things I could imagine: to be excluded and to miss out on the sun.

✦

Waiting for Elyse to reach a developmental milestone is like seven years of waiting for the sun to emerge. When the moment comes, the effect is a ray of sunshine in an otherwise grey world. The golden hour is pure celebration, light. The experience isn't the same with my other children, inhabitants of Earth. They are *expected* to reach milestones. I celebrate them too, of course I do, but it isn't the same. As neurotypical children, they bask in summer light all season long, as every child should, while, societally, Elyse shivers in winter's eternal darkness. With her, I must live all of summer in a day.

✦

I attended a training session with fifteen other parents, the majority of them moms, who had kids with Down syndrome. The goal of our weekend was to be educated in how best to support new parents who've received a prenatal diagnosis of Down syndrome.

"Did you know about the diagnosis before or after birth?" the facilitator asked us. "How did you feel when you found out?"

We threw words onto the chart paper. Grief. Sadness. Loss. Surprise. Anger. The list was overwhelmingly negative. I sat there feeling critical of the instructor, who had a twenty-something-year-old son with Down syndrome. Did she say "Down's kids"? I hated when people did this, as if John Langdon Down were the father of my child. I was overly sensitive to the vernacular, to my insistence on person-first language, an individual *with* Down syndrome. I sat there feeling righteous — we knew beforehand. The facilitator nodded in agreement to the listed feelings we came up with: *yes, these are all normal reactions and feelings to have in response to receiving a Down syndrome diagnosis.*

I raised my hand.

"But isn't that part of why we're here?" I argued. "To hopefully change societal reactions to having a baby born with Down syndrome? To give these parents hope? It's not all bad."

The others looked at me with sad smiles. Some had been crying. The facilitator held my gaze a beat.

I went home that night and nursed Elyse, then passed her off to Dan for storytime. I sat on my bed in our room across the hall, legs crossed, and wrote in my journal. I wrote in long, angry strokes against the page, outraged at how people with Down syndrome were treated and regarded. Without my noticing, an eerie blue light crept into the room through the blinds and beamed through the window directly in front of me, colouring the walls and filling the room with sadness. I stopped writing to examine the light that bathed my lap.

Scattered notes of "Für Elise" floated in through the doorway.

Eventually I stood, walked to the window to look for the cause, and saw only the morose face of the full, shining moon. I was overcome with a heaviness and cloaked in melancholy I hadn't felt since receiving Elyse's prenatal diagnosis. After her birth, I refused to allow any sorrow to seep into my periphery. Two things could not be true at once: I couldn't both love my daughter and be sad that she had Down syndrome, so I chose love.

I collapsed onto the bed. And once I began to cry, a barrage of tears arrived, an endless flow, and I was sobbing, sobbing beneath the blue light. I cried until the blue faded and the sky deepened to dark night.

The facilitator told us the story of when her oldest son got his driver's licence. She felt a sense of pride and accomplishment for her eldest, but also a sense of loss that her younger son with Down syndrome would likely never have the same experience. She labelled this feeling "chronic grief." Grief was born with the initial diagnosis, and this grief resurfaced at will when the parent was reminded of the ways their child was different or missing out. When the facilitator explained this story, I wanted to throw a brick through the window behind me. Why was she telling us these things? Why did the narrative have to remain so overwhelmingly negative?

I have encountered many success stories over the years: adults with Down syndrome who are married, have earned degrees, drive cars, hold down steady jobs, and speak up for themselves. I have my own success stories as a proud parent. Elyse learned to breastfeed after being tube fed for the first two weeks of her life. She could identify the letters of the alphabet before her clever big sister. She surfed in Hawaii with sea turtles and learned a second language. These success stories do not negate the real medical and societal challenges — discrimination, communication, low expectations, ableism — some of which she and our family face every day. The daily challenges exist, and so too do the days when the blue light seeps in and the world feels heavy.

I maintain that "chronic grief" is a depressing description, one that offers a bleak outlook, though it may be accurate and true to lived experience. Just because we don't like or agree with something doesn't mean that it isn't true. Chronic grief does not, however, help me to live and accept the present moment with my daughter.

✦

In the movie version, after the sun retreats and the sky returns to rain clouds, Margot is freed from the closet. Her classmates offered her picked flowers whose buds grew rapidly only once the sun appeared. Her classmates — even the bully — are ashamed for forgetting Margot. Their gestures are ones of atonement. But nothing can replace the sun, can it? Not shame or pity or roses. Bradbury's version forgoes seeking forgiveness. The flower-giving, the actions of remorse, aren't there. Bradbury's story ends with the children awkwardly searching their hands and feet and finally letting Margot out of the room.

✻

Months and months passed after that workshop and the night of the blue light. Life with two young children carried on, as life does. I sat in the nursery, Elyse plopped on my lap, looking away from the window. Soft sunlight pooled on my arm. Elyse was grabbing her books and sliding them onto the floor with her open palm. *Thud, thud.* One after another. She stretched away from me toward the night table, both arms reaching, and I held her snug around her waist with one arm, not paying attention. Staring off into the distance, I went to that place moms go to escape the monotony of child care. Was I calculating which book should be the last story? Ruminating about some perceived slight from the day? Or silently counting down an imaginary timeline before I could leave her room? Did I wonder what I might do with the rest of my evening, the next day, or a week from now? Maybe even daydream about my writing? Or were my thoughts practical, perfunctory: what needs doing? My mind was an endless cartwheel. As I stared at the pink pastel wall, Elyse finally got hold of her music box.

Without my noticing, her thumb and pointer finger kissed in a perfect pincer grasp around the crank's tiny ball handle. And when that first "E" note rang out, I was immediately startled from my reverie and dropped into the present moment. That note was the rising ray of sunlight poking out of the earth and shooting across the sky. That note was the robin's return to announce spring. It was the sound of my heart cracking open, the blue light fading into dispersed mist, and the sun cradled in my lap all at once.

I cried out, "Elyse! It's your song!"

She startled, then looked up over her shoulder at me with a cheeky smile, eyes lit up under her perfectly arched brows. And she kept playing.

I Don't Do Disability

It is not our differences that divide us, it is our inability
to recognize, accept and celebrate those differences.[1]
— Audre Lorde

Nine

I almost quit gymnastics. I am afraid to flip backward, but I have
to flip backward to become a competitive athlete and I haven't been
raised to quit. The girls from my generation are raised to be "good,"
and good means positivity, perseverance, ability. And compliance.
The only honourable option for abandoning sport is injury.

I push off two feet to propel myself backward, throw my arms
up and over my head, and I land on my face. Nose crushed, numb.
Tears rush my eyes from the searing pain; I dab my nostrils for
blood.

"Try it again," my coach yells over.

An older girl crouches down to ask if I'm okay. I tent my hands
over my nose to hide my face and block the tears that fall and run
to the bathroom. *Not broken. Press on. Be good.*

Twelve

By the age of twelve, I can flip high in the air, inverted, body prone, toes pointed to the sky. Floor becomes my best event. My body flows from one end of the rectangular mat to the other, arcing diagonally, scored for its grace and for its dynamic and artistic precision. I compete across the province, once or twice internationally. Gold medals hang heavy around my neck. When I tumble, my body hums with energy and power. I attend a sleepover with the other competitive gymnasts, my friends, at the gym club during the holidays. We eat pizza and candy and flip down the tumble track past midnight, turning, one, two, three, four times on our hands to our feet, tasting freedom, giddy on a sugar high, delirious with our strengths and talents, encouraging and one-upping each other to be better, better, best. "Don't hurt yourselves," our coaches warn, but they don't send us to bed. One a.m., soaring into the night, hands, feet, hands, feet, hands, feet, air, air, air. Sky. Land. Present to the world, arms overhead in a graceful V, fingers fanned. What fun.

I am praised for what my body can do and punished for the mistakes it makes. A bent leg in a bar routine means any number of dips, chin-ups, or leg lifts. Physical conditioning. I learn from my errors quickly, and grow strong, stronger than the boys in my grade six classroom. I grow to respect my body and what it can do. Sore muscles after gruelling five-hour summer practices are a badge of honour. At the end of practice, the sound of gravel crunches beneath my feet. Me and my friends in our colourful bodysuits, ponytails bobbing, jog through the parking lot to cool down, the hot sun pressing on our shoulders. We are warriors, not little girls.

✳

I attend elementary school in the 1990s. My classmates and I sit in rows for friendship assemblies in the gymnasium and sing along to lyrics that roil my tummy with their sickly sweetness. *It's okay to be different!* is the zeitgeist of the times. Adults are good at preaching values, but when it comes to showing how *they* accept differences, many miss the mark. My classmates and I stand up for one fellow student when the supply teacher picks on him for wearing tinted glasses. "Take those off!" the supply shouts. "Who do you think you are, some sort of cool guy?" The supply doesn't let up until our friend is in tears. The student is partially blind, we holler in his defence: *they're prescription!* While our administrators and teachers are onto something with celebrating difference, change — real change — is slow.

At recess time, I sometimes play on the playground with a little boy named Jeremy who has Down syndrome. He is petite for his age, smiley and easy to laugh. His stature makes him look like a kindergartner, but he isn't. Behind his neck smells like fresh soap, and his short, sticky fingers grasp on tight to mine. One recess, Jeremy falls off the play structure ledge onto his face. I happen to be standing nearby, and when I help him to his feet, his stained rosy cheeks are coated with wood chips and tears, a mess of snot and dirt. Jeremy reaches for my neck and tucks his legs up around my waist like a baby koala, while a friend runs for help. He holds on until the teacher arrives to assess his wounds. By then the tears have stopped. I hold him that day. That day, I act like his friend. But the truth is I could just as easily have run away giggling with my friends, free as when I tumbled down those mats.

During indoor recess time, eager to prove my strength, I challenge my classmates to arm wrestles. The girls soon refuse, and the boys put up a fight, but I beat each of them, one at a time. I could be either the nice girl or the fierce competitor.

Weakness was never an option.

Eighteen

I wear tight jeans because that's what's in style. My loose curls are pulled back from my face in a ponytail. I smile at whomever glances in my direction, but I care most about what my friends think. I'm meeting my best friend as she steps off the bus. She comes in from the country on what used to be referred to as a "short bus." Usually, only kids with disabilities ride the short bus. A man named Toby gets off the bus right behind her. And I do mean a man. He has scraggly facial hair, a hunched demeanour, and Coke-bottle glasses atop his googly eyes. My best friend and Toby share the same name and my friend detests this piece of information. Toby is a boy name, she complains.

I can understand why she's upset about the name.

Toby steps past my best friend and hands me a folded note.

"What's this?" I ask him.

"Just ignore him," my friend says, and she keeps walking toward the school.

The note is scrawled in the penmanship of a kindergartner. Toby stands by, making throaty sounds, watching me unfold the note. Inside, three words: *I love you.*

"For you, for you!" he says, pointing at the words, pointing at me.

My best friend is gone, halfway up the large staircase.

"Oh — thank you," I say. I flash him a smile, fold the note into the back pocket of my jeans, and walk away.

The next time I see him, I'm escorting my friend to her bus and Toby rushes to greet me. He passes me another note, this one scrawled with hearts, and reaches in for a hug. Arms outstretched, I pat his shoulders, slouching my body away from touching his.

"He's so annoying! Why do you talk to him?" my best friend asks, rolling her eyes.

"I don't mind — he's sweet," I say, like I'm doing Toby a favour.

Looking back on this scene now, I'm reminded of a stanza in Margaret Atwood's poem "Princess Clothing,"[2] her lines alluding to death and flight. *Oh honey,* the angel-wings version of the afterlife, Atwood is certain, is not how things will go.

Have I romanticized myself in the scene above? Was I pocketing the note to be sweet or to make Toby go away? Do you think I'm sweet? *Oh honey.* I aimed to be perceived a certain way and was bothered that I couldn't fully convince myself of my own goodness. I offered Toby superficial niceness, hollow camaraderie. Why didn't I speak up for him? He was to be tolerated. Tolerance is not enough.

Good people help others; therefore, I am a good person. Throughout high school and into my twenties, I volunteered in daycares, coached children's gymnastics, raked leaves for older generations, and visited a woman with Alzheimer's disease in a retirement home. I mentored children with difficult home lives and taught literacy skills to adults, walked dogs at a local shelter, collected donations for people experiencing poverty, and raised funds by selling lollipops to combat child slavery in India. However, I kept my distance from those with cognitive and physical disabilities. *Why am I volunteering with every group, it seems, except the disabled?* The question nagged at me, disturbed my conscience.

One day, standing on that same stretch of asphalt where Toby had handed me the note, I had an epiphany: *I just don't do disability.* The voice in my head was clear, resolute. What a relief, an immense relief, to acknowledge the negative feelings I'd been wrestling inside, the ones questioning *why* I wasn't volunteering with people with disabilities. With one tidy thought, I was able to dismiss a whole segment of the population. I was able to dismiss the idea that I might one day be disabled or that I had ever been disabled. In honesty, I didn't particularly enjoy working with elderly people, either; children were the light and energy of my life — and what was wrong with that? I knew children could be disabled, but with most programs being inaccessible or segregated at the time, I didn't need to worry about encountering many of those kids. Caring for disabled children was somebody else's responsibility. I viewed disability as a separate construct, and I also viewed disability as a deficit. Inside my head, I had an image of what disability was, and I kept myself and those I loved separate from that category of being. To be disabled was to be weak. Toby and I were in two separate spheres. Or so I thought. *Oh honey, it won't be like that. Not quite.*[3]

⁕

In January 2021, in the midst of the Covid-19 pandemic, I'm watching an online event with author Ziya Tong in conversation with biologist and author Sean B. Carroll at the forty-first edition of the Toronto International Festival of Authors. The banter is lively, engaging, and I'm drawn in. Carroll's book, *A Series of Fortunate Events*, is at the centre of the conversation and he's discussing the role of chance in the creation of life and the universe. How did we even get here? Carroll explains that sixty-six million years ago, an asteroid hit the Earth, ending the dinosaur era and giving rise to the age of reptiles and the beginning of mammals. The event was a one in five-hundred-million-year occurrence, making the chance of humans evolving on planet Earth so minute as to be nothing short of miraculous. "It's been proposed that more than two hundred physical parameters needed to be in place for the existence of life on Earth to arise," concurs Ziya Tong. When it comes to human beings, Carroll says, "We are all each a rare event."

Eight

I'm standing on a parched, grassy field beside my best friend, Trisha, a tall girl with pale skin and freckles, like Anne of Green Gables but with long brown hair. Her mom works at a rehabilitation centre for "handicapped" children. The centre is hosting a special event for its client families with the local minor hockey team, the Peterborough Petes, as special guests.

"Do you want to go?" My mom holds her hand over the receiver, Trisha's mom on the other end.

Do I want to go? I want to go for Trisha. I have little to no sense of what happens at the centre.

The field is a desert. The sun beats down on my neck and I'm sweating, squinting at the sky. Around me, children in motorized chairs with contorted limbs, enlarged foreheads, lolling tongues lie at uncomfortable angles. Their groans float up above the crowd, and someone is squealing with the laughter of a maniacal clown. My friend's mom, or an overly friendly volunteer, hands me a red plastic cup filled with pop. I take the cup, but I know I won't be able to drink or eat anything. The food is tainted. The gathering is meant to be a celebration. The Petes players stand around, hands in their pockets, joking casually with one another, the perfect specimens of what teenage boys "should" be. Balloons are taped to a fold-out table filled with treats. Who is the food for — can these kids even eat it? Is it meant for the siblings, the "regular" kids, like me? Nobody appears to be eating the food, anyway. The table sits in the shadow of the squat handicap centre on the hill. *If I go in there, will I become handicapped too?* The gatherers have congregated in the heat where I am standing. *I don't belong here.* I feel the place looking at me with monster eyes. *I'm not going in there.* I don't want to be here, associating myself with the building or its inhabitants. Microphone feedback grates, and someone official gives a speech. The hockey players are applauded for their charitable efforts.

Looking back, partly I couldn't stand the false cheer of the adults' actions — the pop, the cake, the local celebrities — masquerading as doing these disabled kids a favour and masking the reality of what I believed was their true situation. School and friendships would be difficult, if not impossible.

I stare at a boy in a wheelchair, whose name could be Peter. He's white, average build, with brown hair that drapes across his forehead. He looks "normal" to me, but he's in a wheelchair. I shudder internally, unable to fathom not having the use of my legs. I'm on the precipice of a competitive gymnastics career. What if I couldn't use my legs? I pity the boy mercilessly.

Clown kid steers his mechanical chair closer to me. His head rests back, his eyes askew on his face, like a Cubist painting, teeth sharp and pointy. He's laughing at nothing. *What if that was me? What would I do without my thoughts to keep me company? What would people think of me?* I know these thoughts are wrong, but I also think it's wrong to pretend everything is okay. How could these kids possibly be happy when they can't walk or do well in school? They'll be made fun of. They'll never have a shot at an ordinary life.

I worry clown kid or someone else might reach out and grab me, but nobody does. I do not want their cooties.

"Ready to go, girls?" my friend's mom asks.

Though we've barely arrived, I nod my head vigorously.

"How was it?" my mom asks when I get home.

"Good," I lie.

✻

Ziya Tong asks Sean Carroll, "How many distinct human possibilities can a couple make?" Carroll does the math. *Well, if you take the twenty-three chromosomes from the male sperm and twenty-three chromosomes from the female egg, that's 2^{23} possible chromosomal combinations coming from Dad and 2^{23} possible combinations coming from Mom … and on* he goes, until he arrives at the staggering truth of our uniqueness: "There are more than seventy trillion different combinations."

We are all each a rare event.

36

Twenty-Eight

The first time I truly consider disability, in a meaningful way, is in the hospital when in my arms, I hold my newborn daughter with Down syndrome. Her soft skin and tiny digits curl around my pinky finger. She is everything a baby should be.

To access essential services, I am handed a form with a checkbox beside the word "disabled." The hospital staff wants me to tick off that box. This feels like a test. *But is she disabled?* I wonder. *Aren't all newborns dependent on their mothers? Shouldn't all newborns be considered disabled, then?*

✹

Most of us carry around twenty-three pairs of chromosomes housed in the heart of every cell. People with Down syndrome have one extra chromosome in each cell: forty-seven instead of the typical forty-six.[4] Chromosomes carry our DNA, instructions like whether our eyes will be brown or blue, the tides of our temperament, even our opinions, and whether the stories in this essay matter to the reader — or not.

A genome is the complete set of genetic information in an organism, the entirety of its chromosomes and other genetic material. In people, that includes "all of the approximately three billion base pairs of deoxyribonucleic acid (DNA) that make up the entire set of chromosomes of the human organism."[5] Our environment plays a major role in our outlook, ideas, attitudes, and temperament, but our genome is the blueprint, our physical and metabolic architectural design; the starting point that nurture builds on to make us who we become.

✹

While in a typical pregnancy, up to 20 percent of fetuses are spontaneously aborted, only 20 percent of fetuses with Down syndrome reach full term.[6] That is to say, 80 percent of fetuses with Down syndrome are spontaneously aborted. What does that say about those who survive?

In a 2018 paper titled "The Down Syndrome 'Super Genome,'" published in the journal *Genome Research*, a team of researchers from the University of Geneva and Lausanne hypothesized that the genomes of children with Down syndrome must be "genetically superior" to that of the average person. One researcher, Konstantin Popadin, explains, "The research has shown that for a child with Down syndrome to survive pregnancy and then grow, his or her genome must be of a higher quality so that it can compensate for the disabilities caused by the extra copy of chromosome 21."[7] The conclusion was that the fetuses with Down syndrome that survive have genomes that, outside the additional genetic material of chromosome 21, could be considered genetically close to perfect.

While I was pregnant and blogging every day for Down Syndrome Awareness Month, Dan wrote a guest post[8] — the only piece of writing he's ever written for me. He titled the piece "Superbaby." My favourite line: "Forty-seven chromosomes. A superbaby — awesome!"

Ten

At our school-wide track meet, I place first in the hundred-metre sprint, outcompeting kids older than me. Immediately afterward, I line up to run a second race, twice the distance. I run so hard I think my lungs will burst, and I win again. As I cross the finish line after the final race, two of my best friends are waiting to pass me one of their water bottles. Grateful, I chug the whole thing back in one huge gulp. My friends giggle.

"What?" I ask, smiling, thinking I'm in on the joke.

"That's Jeremy's water bottle!"

Jeremy is the little boy with Down syndrome I sometimes play with.

I throw the water bottle to the ground and wipe my lips clean in disgust.

*

Researcher Stylianos Antonarakis, who led the Super Genome study, explains: "The genome consists of all the genetic material that makes up an individual. It's the genome that determines what becomes of a person and makes him or her grow up and grow old, with or without disease. Some genomes are of better quality than others and can also be less prone to illnesses such as cancer."[9]

One way of measuring the quality of a genome is through the variation in gene expression. The smaller the gene expression variations, the better the genome. "The genome of someone with [Down syndrome] leans towards the average — optimal functioning," says Professor Antonarakis.[10]

Superbaby.

Six

I'm a little girl, sitting poolside in my great-aunt's manicured backyard. The sun is overpowering, the grass a verdant green cut in a crisp line that butts neatly against the concrete. We don't actually go in the pool, and I wonder why. My great-aunt has three sons, and one of them, Jonathan, has Down syndrome. I have memories of only Jonathan; the other two were older and probably didn't stick around. Jonathan, my second cousin, sits with us, but he doesn't speak much. I get the impression he is not allowed. He is difficult to understand. Though he is older, it feels as though he has been relegated to the same status as us children — we are to be seen and not heard.

One thing is clear: Jonathan is peripheral, *other*.

Young children understand what it is to be marginalized.

I wish I could go swimming with Jonathan. He's nice, I think.

My great-aunt doles out balls of a strange orange fruit, and when she offers me one, the sweetness spreads across my tongue: my first taste of cantaloupe. She smiles widely at my brother and me, and looking back now, I wonder if she is overcompensating with that ready smile. *Do I overcompensate with mine now?* The whole set-up is an orchestrated scene, each player treading carefully. My mom plays her part, bringing us to this backyard; my aunt lays out the fruit. They both act as though the other is behind glass. As though what feels real and true, what is left unsaid, would shatter the other. And so we play our parts. I sit calmly, as the dutiful and obedient daughter. My aunt is nice, so nice I wonder why we don't stay longer. My brother and I understand we are not to mention that Jonathan looks or acts different in any way. We are not to comment on "his Down syndrome." We are not to ask questions that may embarrass, which is to say we may ask no questions at all. What is also clear is that Jonathan is loved — but when does love become overbearing? Such was the need to protect him. I understand that need intimately now. *Why do we never stay longer?* The longer we sit in the burning sun, the more I wonder about getting into the pool water to cool off. Our visits are too short for a swim, my mom would argue; short but pleasant. We never stay long and when I press my mom on the issue during the car ride home, her response is close ended. *We don't want to bother them. Be a good girl.*

⁂

One in 1,200. As a twenty-eight-year-old woman, my chance of having a baby with Down syndrome was 1 in 1,200.[11] The incidence of those who have Down syndrome involving a hereditary component is less than 5 percent.[12]

Genetically speaking, if we think of the types of Down syndrome as flowers, 95 percent of cases are wildflowers, uncultivated, appearing randomly, seemingly from nowhere, popping up in the garden completely by chance (known as Trisomy 21). Another 4 to 5 percent are tulips that can involve a hereditary component passed down from generation to generation (called translocation). The last are the fire lilies, incredibly rare, and comprise only 1 percent of cases (mosaicism) where the cells' chromosomal makeup is mixed.[13]

From a small sample of her DNA, Elyse's genome was karyotyped after her birth. The image of her chromosomes, although we didn't see it, looked like pairs of dancing coral. Elyse was categorized as a wildflower, garden-variety Trisomy 21. No hereditary component. Her extra chromosome happened by chance.

Our species's survival depends on adaptation. Difference. Change. Sean Carroll explains, "For change to happen, there has to be variation in a species. There are thirty or forty mutations that weren't there in our parents, out of three billion letters in our DNA. Mutation is just variation. This is a built-in feature of DNA. Spontaneous mutations take place. It's a feature, not a bug. That's chance working. With no mutation, there would be no evolution."

Thirty

Before she could walk, when Elyse was a toddler of two-and-a-half years old and Ariel was four, I flew to India to attend the World Down Syndrome Congress.

What will it be like to meet people with Down syndrome from around the world? At this point, I had spent time with other babies and children with Down syndrome, and a handful of adults with disabilities, but I had never heard a person with Down syndrome speak up for themselves, and I didn't expect to.

Petite in stature, with neatly trimmed hair that fell below her collarbone and round, red-rimmed glasses, Shéri stood behind the podium at the front of the room, the honoured speaker, and talked about her life as a woman with Down syndrome. With pain in her voice, she recounted the tragic death of her father, who had died from a fall while reaching for his cellphone, which had slipped from his hands. Shéri lightheartedly recalled the boys who made fun of her in elementary school. She threatened to give them her Down syndrome. "That kept them quiet," she said. She was named "Woman of the Year" in South Africa after becoming the first qualified teacher in the world with Down syndrome.[14] But it was her plea for her own life that grabbed at my heart and mind and has never let go since.

"People like me are aborted," she said, looking directly out at the crowd. "We deserve to live."

Her words boomed like mountain echoes, and in the moment following, nobody moved, nobody breathed.

I thought I was going to India to help people. I would take what I'd learned and bring that knowledge back to other parents in the Down syndrome community and, by extension, help children with Down syndrome. I'd pictured facts, methods, neat graphs, and statistics. Medical information. I did come home with that information from the conference, but the greatest learning came from the individuals with Down syndrome themselves, and the felt experience of being there. Shéri's speech ushered in a new wave of thinking. I was learning, as one delegate quoted St. Benedict, to listen with the ear of my heart. Shéri and other conference delegates lived full, meaningful lives. They were loved and received love in return. I had significantly more to learn from Shéri than she had to learn from me, in that moment. And she was giving me a glimpse of what was possible for my daughter. I hadn't realized how desperately I needed to see such a role model. Shéri's words — *we deserve to live* — cut through me to something larger, deeper. She reached for a broader understanding within me, an understanding I was only beginning to grasp with the ear of my heart but could not yet fully comprehend. I had yet to find the words.

⁂

I write to ask Gregory Mansfield — who is a lawyer, wheelchair user, and disability-rights activist in the U.S. — why he chooses to call himself "a disabled person" versus "a person with a disability," and he graciously takes the time to respond:

> I think it is the prerogative of each person to choose whether they prefer person-first or identity-first language. I prefer identity-first language for a couple reasons. First, disability is my identity and I see nothing wrong with being disabled or having a disability. Next, I don't need to be reminded or remind others that I'm a person. Many people who use person-first language seem to feel the need to emphasize that they are a person first and [it] relegates or deemphasizes disability as a negative. Again, to me, disability is not a negative thing. It is part of my identity.
>
> Having said all of this, there is no right answer. A disabled person, and only the disabled person, should decide how they want to be identified. Nondisabled people, including family members, should never tell disabled people how to identify.

Amanda Leduc, who on her website identifies as "a disabled writer and author," recounts having her own realization about person-first language, but in regard to herself as a writer with cerebral palsy. In an interview with *Quill & Quire*, Leduc recalls arguing with an employer who said she would one day be known as a disabled writer. "I said, 'No, I'll be a writer with a disability.' I didn't want my disability to be the first thing that people thought of when they saw me. And that's internalized ableism."[15]

Thirty-Four

My friend Emily and I are visiting a group of school children. Their eyes light up when they see Emily in her rhythmic gymnastics bodysuit. With perfectly pointed toes, accuracy, and grace, she tosses balls and manipulates hoops and dangles ribbons. I am in awe of her. Her red hair flashes when she spins. Emily is a year older than I am and still sliding into the splits. My presentation is about Down syndrome and kindness. Emily speaks to her lived experience as a woman with Down syndrome and recalls her world travels as a Special Olympics athlete. She talks about her job at Boston Pizza and about volunteering at a respite home for families who have children with disabilities. She brings in her Olympic gold medals for the kids to admire; they run their fingers over the embossing with reverence.

I tell students the story of Jeremy, the little boy with Down syndrome, and how my friends handed me his water bottle after my race. I ask the kids: what could I have done differently? What would have made the situation better?

Their answers are measured and thoughtful, practical and kind. "You could bring your own water bottle," a grade one student suggests, or "Go fill the water bottle back up and give it back to the boy," offers another. To them, this isn't hard. One grade eight student remarks, indignant, "Get better friends."

I met Emily at a BBQ run by our local Down syndrome association and we related to one another. She's easygoing in a way I could never be. I feel instantly comfortable around her. Early on in our friendship, we give a talk together to college students.

Emily presents the same materials about her life, and I talk about Down syndrome and becoming a parent advocate. From the look on Emily's face, I suspected my stories were boring. She sits in the front row, eyes drooping. I make a mental note to ask her how it went afterward.

A question-and-answer period remains at the end of our talk. One student asks when a person "gets" Down syndrome.

I answer confidently, "At the moment of conception. When sperm meets egg."

On the car ride home, I nervously turn to my friend for feedback. Had I talked for too long? Was the presentation interesting?

"Well, how did it go, Em?" I ask her. "How did I do?"

"Well," Emily reflects a moment before answering, "you talked a lot about sperm!"

"*What?*" I'm perplexed. Is she joking?

"Too much sperm."

And now I'm laughing and Emily's laughing because I remember the student's question and my answer: *when sperm meets egg.*

I value Emily's feedback. The rest of my presentation, I discern, was somewhat dry.

During one coffee date with Em, she mentions volunteering at the respite home that day. She was supposed to help feed a child in a wheelchair, but he was drooling and so she didn't want to do it.

"He was so disgusting," Em says, twisting her face.

When I point out he probably couldn't help it, she doesn't budge on her stance. "It was gross."

In talking with her mom afterward, I bring up the conversation. Her mom shakes her head. "Yes, we've talked to her about these kinds of things before. She can be quite judgmental. You would think she'd have more empathy."

When I run this scene past Emily, she scrunches up her face and asks, "What does 'judgmental' and 'empathy' mean?"

We talk about each word and then look up synonyms on her electronic spellchecker, which unfortunately does nothing to help with the understanding of the words. But fortunately, in doing so, we come across the word "censorious" for "judgmental," which invokes a kind of delight in us both, and isn't that part of the point? To delight in one another's company? To revel in the design of the other, no matter the count of our chromosomes, the architectural design of our cells? To marvel and consider a person for what they are: a work of art.

"I would never have said that to the boy," Em says. "I would just have asked someone else to do it."

"That's a fair point, Em," I say. "I'll add that in."

"I could never have been a doctor," she adds. "I would have thrown up. I mean, I can give somebody a Band-Aid or something."

Twenty-Eight

I'm standing on the sandy island shores of Barbados and looking out at the Caribbean Sea. The heaving waves mimic the amniotic fluid and movements of the baby I am carrying inside me. Waves rolling over. Again and again. And the grief. Two days ago, I found out I am carrying a fetus with Down syndrome. I grieve the loss of the typical baby I'm expecting, and a slew of emotions passes through me. In a moment of euphoria, a burst of positive energy, *I have it!* I know what I will do with this new life my baby is giving me. My destiny is to teach children with Down syndrome. *Maybe I will even open a school for kids with Down syndrome. Do kids with Down syndrome even go to regular schools?* In that moment, on the beach, I'm not sure, but it doesn't matter. *Those poor babies with Down syndrome*, I think; *I'm going to save every last one of them.*

I wrote this scene in my unpublished memoir as a moment of hope, the beginning of my journey to acceptance and personal transformation as a mother, but now I look at it differently. I look back at that scene as a point of comparison between who I am today and what I believed then, as plot points on the pathway to acknowledging my own ableism.

*

During her talk with Emily Urquhart, "Making Room for Disability: Mining Folklore and Fairytales," at the 2020 Wild Writers Literary Festival, disabled author Amanda Leduc said, "Why can't we just celebrate our differences? As a society, why can't we just *do* disability?"

Thirty-Six

Every day of my life is now coloured with a disability lens. I am a parent disability advocate, and that is the perspective I speak from. I don't currently consider myself disabled. I have the use of my legs, fair eyesight, my full faculties, but that could change and, as I age, likely will. Disability is a spectrum. At times, I am temporarily disabled. When I become ill or catch a flu and can't get out of bed, or when I sprain my ankle, for example. And the way I couldn't see — the not-seeing of — my own ableism is in itself a sort of disability. My hope is to continue to grow and learn and to one day look back on this essay and shake my head at what I do not yet know intimately. Some things I may never know, no matter how hard I try, but I'm listening — as St. Benedict put it, listening with the ear of my heart.

Temporary or permanent, hidden or visible, disability is part of the human condition. As Amanda Leduc put it during her talk at Wild Writers, "Disability is everywhere." I have disabled friends and a daughter with disabilities, and it is their experiences and voices that are helping to guide me through and away from my own ableism.

Twenty-Eight

On the fourth day of Elyse's life, she was in the neonatal ICU and I couldn't hold her. My milk came in and the need for the weight of her tiny body in my arms was visceral, primal, but she was two days post abdominal surgery, and the placement of her breathing tube was precarious. We couldn't risk moving her and ripping it out, causing her more pain. When I walked in to see her that morning, she was so drugged up on pain medication that she looked dead. The breathing tube was part of what was keeping her alive. Her limbs lay useless by her sides. I immediately left the room and went to the downstairs lobby to cry, as my breasts throbbed with yearning. The respiratory therapist, who had been working with us, saw me crying in Dan's arms; when I came back upstairs to Elyse's room, she was standing beside the nurse on duty.

"We're going to let you hold her," she said.

With Herculean effort, managing the tubing and delicate apparatus, they wrapped Elyse in a flannel blanket and found a place for her in my arms. I was the happiest mother on Earth that day. I mean, *what are the chances?*

And I have held her since and never let go — never once let go of my baby who was born exactly as she should be.

＊

One in 500 million. Seventy trillion. One in 1,200. Only 20 percent of fetuses with Down syndrome reach full term.

Perhaps Elyse, our superbaby, my wildflower, was never meant to live an ordinary life. It took a series of fortunate events for her to become my daughter and arrive safely in my arms. *We are all each a rare event.* The likelihood of her being here is extraordinarily rare.

WOMAN

Everyday Devotion

I HANG UP the phone. I've been on the phone a while.

Dan walks in from his run and I immediately challenge him. "What is this still doing here?"

He stares at me and remains mute, a porcupine that's stumbled out of the brush into a bear: my nostrils are flared, eyes menacing and large.

"I asked you to put this away, *why didn't you clean up, why didn't you put this away, you said you would put this away!*"

And now the empty suitcase — the one that held his belongings for the summer, which have long since been packed away into dresser drawers — is flying, flying, careening across the room in my husband's direction. I miss him completely, and the bag lands with a dramatic *thump*. I let out a growl and stamp my feet on my way out of the cottage, slamming the door behind me. I storm down to the lake and stand at the edge of the dock in the high, glaring sun, arms crossed, back turned on my family.

I catch sight of my watch. *Shit.* It's already noon, time for my virtual weekly writers' group. I make my way back inside to my laptop.

I'm not sure I want to be here, but I sign on anyway. I'm raw from my outburst, and the greetings and pleasantries I dole out to the other participants feel false. I despise myself for putting up such a front to other truth-tellers, to my tribe of writers.

Jason, the group's facilitator, posts a writing prompt and then for twenty minutes we sprint to complete a piece of writing. We write in our notebooks, facing the darkened Zoom screen, cameras off, against time and ourselves and whatever doubts we carry within. When the timer chimes, Jason brings us back together and we share what we've written, if we want to.

The act of expunging my thoughts should make me feel better, but I'm hesitant. Something is wrong. *Why don't I want to lean into that pain?*

The prompt of the day comes from a random word generator. We have five arbitrary words and twenty minutes to work with. *Inch, register, poison, produce, throw.*

The piece I write begins weirdly.

> ***Inch*** *closer to freedom.* I'm cloistered in the small cottage I'm living in for the summer with my family. We'll be moving back to a bigger space soon, although our three kids going back to school will give me more freedom than the changing of spaces. ***Register*** *for my retreat.* I'm running a writers' retreat and I'm hopeful my writers' group members will join — blatant advertising. ***Poison*** *the frog that licks you back.* My youngest daughter was recently poisoned from holding toads and not washing her hands properly afterward. She spent two separate evenings vomiting. I wrote a blog post about it, "The Curious Incident of the Frog in the Night."

Throw away the trash, clear the cobwebs from your *life*. And in effect, that is what I am doing with these first few sentences, clearing the cobwebs from my mind, pulling up a blank page for the possibility of truth-telling.

A thinly veiled cloak of calm pleasantries. My writing group sits on the other side of their screens, discussing their practice, their craft, their success, their vacation, their struggles to focus but in the confines of a day with actual time.

Afterward, when I read this to them out loud, one will remind me she is working full time as a nurse, seventy-plus-hour weeks, and another — also in support, not as a complaint — will remind me he deals with depression and misses out on at least a few full days of writing each month. I'm reminded that my struggles are not unique, they are simply my own.

I'm suffocating. Drowning. I don't want to write; I want to scream. Throw the laptop. I threw a suitcase in my husband's direction today.

I want all the things without having to look after them. I want the cottage and a husband who can fix things, who fixes me. I want three children who will look after themselves. I want a dog who will train himself. Even the dog turned on me, baring his teeth.

I continue writing, and the piece transforms into what's been hiding underneath. I write my way there. Mostly, I want a better ending — for my daughter and me — than the one my great-aunt had with her son.

My mom called me this morning to let me know my great-aunt died — and that, because of Covid restrictions, she did not want me to attend the funeral. My great-aunt was mother to Jonathan, my second cousin with Down syndrome. I respect my mom's wishes and won't push the issue. Maybe that's why I'm mad. This denial of my grief, of our collective grief.

My great-aunt who has died, she did everything for her son Jonathan, a man in his forties with Down syndrome and early-onset Alzheimer's, and now she's gone. She was eighty-three years old. Nobody should have to be a caregiver to their child until eighty-three. She brushed his teeth, helped him into his pyjamas. He can't go places by himself because he may get lost or hurt, taken advantage of. Because he forgets. Who will take care of him now? Does anybody even care?

What a sneaky thief grief is, robbing us of our joyful days.

My great-aunt left behind a husband and three sons. I have a husband and three daughters.

Who will look after Jonathan now?

Not knowing what to do, but wanting to do something, I wrote a note on my aunt's virtual wall of memories, set up by the funeral home. Mine was one of two comments. In my note, I wrote that my aunt was kind to me; she was good. She hosted us in her backyard, poolside, when I was a child; gave me my first taste of cantaloupe. She lived a life of servitude.

When I visited her last, I didn't mean to judge her, but I couldn't help but wonder, who would take her place to care for Jonathan when she was gone? She had done too much. She had enabled him. It wasn't her fault — she was a product of the time she grew up in, the people around her. My people. Our family.

I want closure. A chance to give Jonathan a hug and his dad's hand a squeeze. A chance to connect with family rarely seen.

My mom asked me not to come. She was her aunt. What am I supposed to say?

And that's where the piece ends. Time up. I turn my camera back on as the basin of tears overflows.

Now, I don't believe my great-aunt enabled Jonathan, her son. When I last visited her a few years ago, as part of my research when I was writing a memoir about giving birth to my own daughter with Down syndrome, she answered my questions, one by one, as best she could, and it was she who wanted me to know, "He used to be able to do more …"

Sitting in the chair across from her, as a young mom I embodied hope for the future, and for my daughter with Down syndrome and what she would one day be able to do; Jonathan's faculties had been stolen from him. I quickly intuited that for my aunt, the experience of losing who her son had been was not easy to relay in the face of such optimism. She was hesitant to speak, like she was painting a picture she didn't want me to see.

"He used to take the bus, until he got lost a few times and ended up at the wrong stop."

When I spoke to Jonathan directly, asking him questions, my great-aunt answered for him, several times.

Early-onset Alzheimer's, a disease of memory, robbed him of his independence; not Down syndrome, not his mother. These are important distinctions for me to make. He had been taking the bus regularly; his faculties were fading. His mother stepped in, saved his life. Sacrificed her own.

Is that fair to say? That she sacrificed her life for her son; that we, as mothers, sacrifice our own lives for our children? In many ways, we certainly do. In this case, the adult child needed a caregiver, and his mother accepted that role. Was this her burden, her cross to bear, or one of the greatest joys of her life? Who is to know? Who is to judge? Why do I think this situation calls for judgment? Why does *she* need to be judged? What was Jonathan's father's role in caregiving? My great-uncle was a loving presence in the home, but even when I was a child and our families got together, he remained absent or in the background. Why is it a mother's responsibility to look after the children? Why are mothers the only ones judged for their parenting? Judgment feels more like an end than a beginning.

One definition of an "end," in the *Oxford Dictionary*, is "a person's death,"[1] whereas a "beginning," as a noun, is simply "the point in time or space at which something starts."[2] A conversation, maybe. Empathy, perhaps? Beginnings leave room, in other words, whereas judgment is like death: swift and unforgiving. I fear I have judged her too harshly. That I will also be judged for what I have done or haven't done. In this essay, my great-aunt deserves a new beginning.

In Chloe Caldwell's book of essays, *I'll Tell You in Person*, Caldwell recounts the story of her piano teacher, who made her do everything over and over until she could do it seven times in a row, correctly. "If you do something seven times in a row correctly, you never forget it,"[3] the piano teacher explained.

I repeat the words in my head out loud seven times. *Judgment feels like more of an end than a beginning.* I remind myself not to judge others; I remind myself not to judge myself. I don't want to forget.

I want to believe that I can free myself from making judgments about others and, in turn, free myself from caring when it comes to their judgments about me. How will I judge myself for the decisions I make about my daughter? For the time I devote to her care? *She did too much; she didn't do enough.*

At thirty-six years old, I don't want to have children in my care forever. Of course, I will care for them, but that is different from having them *be in* my care. I don't see how co-dependency is in either of our best interests — but hold on, is this not a judgmental statement? My children, like all children, will depend on me forever, as I depend on my mother and vice versa. I'm their mom. A fellow mom of a child with Down syndrome once said to me, "I didn't have children not to love them for their whole lives." What parent wouldn't give of themselves for the ones they love? What set of circumstances is ideal?

In our North American society, creating an independent child is touted as the ultimate goal of the successful parent. My great-aunt loved her son for her whole life, and most of his. He was in her care until the moment she died. This isn't a situation easily judged by an outsider.

What was it, the erratic flutter in her chest, a hardening, a tingling, a cessation of blood flow — at what point did she know she was dying of a heart attack, and what did she think about, in her final moments? Were her thoughts for her adult son? For her husband, her partner in life, for their three boys as a whole? Or in the end, did she take that moment for herself, her last breath, with the grace of release?

In the end, isn't she just like me, putting one foot in front of the other? *How did I get here?* One delicate step at a time. We wind our way to the end and are either mindful of our movements or resigned to our fates. Was each day a rushing current, pulling my great-aunt downriver, or a gentle stream from which you cup both hands, bend over, and take a drink? I hope that my great-aunt drank fully of this life; she reminds me to plunge right in. Not everyone lives for happiness; we are not all slaves to the master of a hedonistic existence: I have to remind myself of this. There are those called to a higher power of being, to that of serving others, but most of us are everyday people. Everyday people with two feet falling one in front of the other, trying not to trip and land on our faces, get dragged down by the current. "Attention is the beginning of devotion,"[4] Mary Oliver wrote. We think of those who are caregivers until the end as saints, but my great-aunt wasn't Mother Teresa — she was a mother engaging in everyday devotion.

✳

When I turn on my camera to rejoin my writing group, my tear-stained face and jagged breath hushes any conversation, their care evident. I read. I cry my way through telling the story of my great-aunt, feeling every bit of her loss without closure. I have written my way into a closure of my own by having others bear witness to my pain caused by her death, to my pain caused by the loss of the magnitude of her love shown in her everyday devotions. *Will that be me one day?* Of course, I can't help but wonder. The tears from my upper eyelids fall down onto the page.

And maybe, in the end, what I want is just to be seen. To have my feelings heard and acknowledged; I want to have some say in how I get to live out my own life.

✳

Later that afternoon, I'm sitting by myself at the end of our dock in a red plastic Muskoka chair, facing the lake. The water is quiet and I am still, exhausted from emotion. Elyse appears from behind, then stands in front of me with her hands on my shoulders and leans in for a kiss. She doesn't say anything. She doesn't have to.

Later, the kids in bed, my husband and I make our way down to a blazing fire I've built in our firepit beside the lake. As soon as I got off the call with my writers' group, I told him about my reading, about understanding my anger that morning, and why I had wept.

"I know," he says. "I knew why you were mad this morning."

"You did? I'm sorry," I tell him.

A warm glow emits from the circle of rocks and lights our cheeks orange. I sit on my husband's lap and he comforts me under the cloak of night, slides his hand down and presses where it feels good. I rest my head back into the crook of his neck. The sky is clear, and we look up at a web of stars. From the farmer's field down the lake, the faint sound of cowbells rings in the distance; their chiming mingles with the din of our neighbours' voices, their laughs, and somewhere, the familiar sound of The Tragically Hip, that guitar twang of "Bobcaygeon," and the stellar reveal.

"I love this song," I say.

"I hate the Tragically Hip," he replies.

"I know you do."

My behaviour from earlier is forgotten; instead of judgment, he gives me love. And a new beginning.

A Loon

WHEN THE PANDEMIC hits, the first thing my family does is buy a dog; the second thing we do is buy a cottage. The dog is something we can enjoy, a cheerful distraction, a welcome addition to our family. The cottage is meant to be a place of refuge, a way to escape everyday life and shelter from the storm. We don't expect the storm will follow. That we will become the storm.

We don't just buy the cottage — we move there, rent out our house. This acquisition, I acknowledge, is an immense privilege; shame is not lost on me when it doesn't quite work out. We migrate to our new home like birds in the summer flocking north.

The day we move into the cottage, the nature gods send an omen. Two loons, notoriously shy birds, perch together on the end of our dock, leaning into one another like lovers. As the light gives way to night, I usher the children from their beds. Ariel is nine, Elyse seven, and Penelope is three, about to turn four. They take turns, one by one, looking at the loons through the antique binoculars left behind by the previous owner. From our cottage set into the hill, we ooh and ahh, standing at the small wooden balcony off the living room that overlooks the lake. Loons, aquatic birds, are like elegant, oversized mallards dressed in their finest evening wear. Ruby eyes and a black-and-white-checkered pattern along their backs; their movements are lithe and measured in the way of creatures who know survival. You would never try to pet one — such is their wildness. I see the loons' presence as a sign of good things to come. Through the viewfinder, we can clearly see the distinct necklace of pearls, the midnight feathers. Auspicious beginnings, indeed.

I watch the lovers' dance of the loons through June, July, and into August. They expertly glide across the lake's surface, leisurely paddling to and fro. They make an exquisite pair; they make being a loon look easy.

Before the pandemic hit, my husband and I were like that, gliding along in unison in our marriage. Our lives were hectic, but with a semblance of order and predictability. Before the pandemic, when we had other places to go, no amount of time together could feel wrong. Before, we had a chance to swim apart. The forced seclusion of the cottage became a sort of drowning in each other.

Loons are expert fishers and can dive down as deep as two hundred feet to catch their prey.[1] One and then the other. They hunt for fish, frogs, crayfish, mussels, leeches, and various aquatic insects.[2] They are self-sufficient, and I believed so was I.

Pre-pandemic, Dan and I regularly spent time apart, as he travelled often for work — a night, a week, ten days — then reunited, grateful for the return of the other. A group of loons is called a cry or an asylum — not words I associate with peace of mind. Space and time to oneself can be a good thing. I grew used to Dan's absences for work, almost fond of them. In his daytime departures, while the kids were at school, I found quiet and solitude — not so bad for a writer. I found a rhythm in caring for our three children that, over time, got easier on my own. You can grow used to anything. The nest wasn't empty — he was coming back, though I often missed having someone to talk to once the kids were asleep.

The cottage living space is one large room with a screened-in porch. Three bedrooms line up cozily up along the back. Large bay windows span its front width and look out over the lake and the beautiful vista of white pines and hilly terrain. The setting is almost too idyllic. The glossy exterior is a facade.

On the surface, the loon's demeanour appears calm, but below water, webbed feet paddle furiously.

Over the summer months, with no day programs, summer camps, extracurricular activities, or teenage babysitters, and limited contact with grandparents to take shifts with the children, our relationship suffers. I am trying to work full time; he is trying to work full time.

I look up from my desk to where the kids are playing by the water, and shout across the room: "Who's responsible for the kids right now?" I keep my eyes trained on them. "I thought you were," I accuse, before he can answer. One of the kids steps onto the forbidden dock. I stand.

"No, when we talked about it, it was you," he says. His reply is foreboding — if the issue is pressed further, we will argue about it.

I slam my fists onto the desk and head out the door. I walk across the side deck, hop the two steps to the ground and scream at the kids, *"Get away from the water."* I wave my arm violently in the universal sign of *come here.* "Get *off* the dock *now* — we told you *never* to go on the dock. *Get inside."*

The girls come running. I see only the tops of their heads as they scoot past.

With loons, the male and female both contribute to building the nest.[3]

I come back inside, letting the screen door slam behind me.

Dan says nothing.

✹

Before the pandemic, a happy marriage looked like our Sunday mornings. Holding each other beneath the sheets before the kids woke up, blocking the door with a basket full of dirty laundry. One last quick kiss on the lips — sometimes deeply — before I would shut the door behind me to go for a run, and the smell of fried oil that greeted me when I returned. The eggs, bacon, and crepes the kids helped him cook. Soft afternoons, slanted light pouring through the window and us folding laundry together on the bed where we made love.

At the cottage, Dan and I find ourselves in a place of bitter standstill.

"Things have changed," I remind him. "You don't understand what this is like for me."

After nine years of looking after our children, this was supposed to be my time to focus on being a graduate student, a writer; my summer to work, build a new career. "You need to support me."

We draw inside ourselves for solace, focusing on our own needs that are not being met. Dan has always been giving of his time; it's hard for me to understand this shift away from who I thought he would be in this time of crisis and change. Is he feeling the same way? Meanwhile, our three children wander aimlessly along the rim of the lake, collecting frogs in the marsh, throwing sticks, killing time. As the summer wears on, they spend the time outdoors idly, and without ceremony, to be free of us and the tension.

We hear the loons wailing at night. This is the proper term: "the wail."[4] Long, hollow calls echo across the lake, both forlorn and enchanting. To us, the wails carry no meaning, but to the loons, they have lost each other. They call out, ceaseless, looking to make contact, to find one another and reunite with their lost mate, sometimes their missing children.

✦

"Why are you acting this way?"

I'm curled on my side on our grey, dilapidated couch, breath-catching-in-throat sobbing as Dan stands brooding off to the side. He says something, but I can't — won't — hear him. We've been fighting for what feels like hours.

"You're being such an asshole. Leave me alone." I abruptly get up and push past him into the bathroom.

He would never physically harm me, I know this, and yet he keeps his distance as if holding himself back; as if I'm fire burning, and if he touches me, we'll ignite.

I duck behind the sheer shower curtain, imprinted with moose and smores and campfires and all the cottage fun we're not having in this moment. I cover my ears, press the heels of my hands into my eyes, but the tears won't stop flowing. What is this fight about? I don't even know anymore.

He stands in the doorway, a dark silhouette behind the thin barrier.

"You're acting like a *child*," he hisses at me, and I can feel the deadness in his eyes, their light extinguished by hurt.

"Just leave me alone. Leave me alone, leave me alone." Those are the only words I know. I have no fight left in me, no other vocabulary to erase the pain.

Later that afternoon, I get in the car and drive the five minutes into town. I leave. I've been wanting time to write and now I have it. I sit on the back patio, masked and alone, at the only café in town, staring at the blank screen of my laptop, devoid of words, drained from the emotional strain. I wanted to leave, and so I left. And now I have nothing to say for myself. I'm too astonished at the depths of our anger.

Each time we argue and the walls of our marriage weaken, I'm left feeling exposed and I try to hide. I curl up in a ball on my side and pull the bedsheets over my head. I sink into myself the way loons get low in the water under stress. I squeeze my eyes shut as the tears pour onto the bathroom floor behind the shower curtain. I cover my ears, but I can't escape the tearing sound in my chest. When things get bad between us, the thin walls of the cottage press in too tightly, collapse.

My heart wails.

*

Of course, we also have days of joy, laughter, and love. Hikes in Algonquin Park with the dog; a handful of family visitors, swimming in the lake, campfires, and the constant surround sound of nature: birds chirping, birch leaves rustling high above, and tiny waves lapping rhythmically against the shore. The highs become an affront to the lows. The sun will bronze our skin, the wind tangle our hair, and laughter and bird calls will ring out, but we will remain utterly lost from each other. We've lost the rhythm of love in our exchanges.

"I'm trying to support you," he says.

I believe him. I just don't feel it.

Our family survives the summer. The kids return to school, and this is the exhale and break we truly need. Despite my love for the cottage, after six months of having our children home, the end of August can't come soon enough.

*

In mid-September, I return to the cottage on my own to run a virtual writers' retreat. I leave my family members behind, except for the dog.

On the day I arrive, a single loon sits at the end of our dock, huddled into itself.

I stand on our small balcony, admiring the solitary bird — just the one. *Where did your partner go?* I wonder. *Do you feel lonely?*

I felt lonely. Even among my family, day in and day out, in our one-room cottage, I felt isolated, and isolation feels lonely. I felt some of the loneliest feelings I've ever felt. That loon and I had something to say to one another.

The online retreat I organize is about time and space to write, but it's also about connection, wellness, bringing women writers together. I ask my cousin Lindsey, a yoga teacher, to run a virtual yoga session that includes meditation and journalling, on the opening morning of the retreat. Though I am the weekend's facilitator, I decide to participate in this session too, Zoom camera off.

Our bodies flow in choreographed movements, and we open our hearts, chests proud. We lie on our mats on the ground, palms open to the ceiling, and Lindsey takes us on a memory story walk. She asks us to picture ourselves at different time points, beginning in childhood. And there I am, two years old, toddling across my parents' front lawn, on the green grass beside the red-brick home I grew up in, pink geraniums in the garden, summertime, moving toward an adult's open arms; and at age nine, learning to tumble and fall at gymnastics practice, nineties brown bangs kissing my eyebrows.

I find myself in a dream-like state, a mindset similar to floating on my back in the lake and looking up at the clear blue sky. I feel that uncertainty of where the sky ends and the water begins, my body floating somewhere in between.

Perhaps what causes me to break down is that, in this meditative state, I am not alone.

Lindsey asks us to envision a "benevolent being," which she describes as someone who is well-meaning and kind to you. A person who has your best intentions at heart. I interpret this description as a feeling of unconditional love. During each memory she walks us through, our benevolent being is with us.

I could have chosen my mom or dad, but without a question, my benevolent being is my husband. Dan is the one my mind calls forth, and his presence, his feelings of love — as he watches me fall as a little girl and laughs kindly at my pluckiness — my cousin's warmth and words, her familiarity, and his love bring me to tears. I'm lying on the cottage floor in the middle of my writers' retreat, camera off, and I am wailing. I'm wailing because my husband loves me, and I am not a solitary bird.

He loves me, but we have lost each other. Isolating together in one space with three small children to look after, with myriad needs, has pushed us apart. Whichever one of us was free of responsibility left the burden of care to the other. The abandoned children, the unruly dog, the second home. It was only the two of us performing three full-time jobs. Countless responsibilities, with no reprieve, and we were burned out, taking on too much. And we were resentful of the other.

I lie there, sobbing, because I feel his love wash over me, and I love him back. Nothing has changed between us. We are safe. We are one, and we are whole.

With the guided meditation complete, I sit up and wipe away my tears, dry my cheeks, and pick up my pen. We are to write a reflection of our experience. I feel as though I have awakened from another world, like I have come crashing to the surface from somewhere deep below, gasping for breath.

Lindsey has one last surprise for us.

"Normally, in person," she explains, "I would draw a Tarot card for each of you at the end of class, so we'll do that now."

One person's spirit animal is a lion. Someone else, I believe, is given a pig. She draws my card last: The Loon.

Lindsey reads the meaning of the card: "A solitary bird of the wilderness that symbolizes tranquility, servitude, and the awakening of old hopes and dreams. A loon relies on water — a symbol for dreams and multiple levels of consciousness."

When my husband and I envisioned our lives together, we didn't picture the hardships, but they were waiting, just below the water's edge. Troubled times are as inevitable as those perfect days with still waters and pristine pine reflections on the lake's surface. We are two lucky loons gliding along into the sunset — until we're not. But our love has layers, depth. His love can find its way into my meditations, my visions, and dreams, even when I've forgotten about it, placed it elsewhere.

I needed to be alone to see that.

On the second day of the retreat, standing at the end of the dock, my dog by my side, an orb torpedoes underwater right in front of me. At first I think it's a turtle, but it darts by quickly in a choreographed movement. I keep my eye on the water. Fifty feet out, a shadow emerges, then disappears. I stare out at the waves a few minutes more until a faint figure appears far across the lake. Is there one loon or two? Hard to say.

The loons' eerie calls, echoing through the night, have stayed with me long past the summer months, the way I am haunted by those darker moments in our marriage during the pandemic.

But now that we've sunk to that place, I know no matter how deep down I go in search of sustenance, survival, he will be right there, swimming by my side, urging me on with his love, plunging into the deep dark with me.

Loons mate for life.

How to Make New Love

THE SUMMER DAN disappeared was the first summer of the pandemic. Physically, he was present, but other parts of him that I knew and loved and depended on shut down. He moved through our newly acquired cottage, the place we'd settled into for the summer, with a frazzled discontent. We had expected ourselves to be able to work full time, look after three children, train a new puppy, live the cottage life, and be productive in the confines of a small space. His work consisted mostly of conference calls. Mine involved deep concentration. Once, at least once, Elyse streaked naked behind his chair while he was on a video call with physicians. We expected too much of ourselves and neither of us wanted to take responsibility. Neither of us wanted to admit to our fears — *how long will this last?* — and our perceived failures: *we need help*. And so we argued — fiercely.

The turmoil that rose in our relationship was like waves crashing against the shoreline, wearing down the rock.

The collective expectation — let's call it the Hallmark greeting card version of love — is that the longer two people are together, as years pass, the stronger love will grow. As a young girl, I assumed love strengthens in the way that one naively hopes one's parents will be around forever. Why else would two people stay together? Who wants to commit to something long term that doesn't get better with time, or *at least* stays the same?

But what happens, as it did that summer, when the flow of love sputters, slows to a trickle, freezes completely — does that mean the relationship must end?

Slogans of wisdom come in contradictory pairs; the counter-argument is that love fades over time. I often hear this as an unsound argument for why a woman should stay with a partner she no longer loves. *You can't expect that love you had to last forever!*, a questionable friend might quip. But what about when it doesn't end, or doesn't need to end; I find myself wondering: does love fade or simply transform into something new?

That summer, our choreographed movements, the dance of our distress, eroded the rock of our marriage, turning it into something less solid, like the mossy lichen wearing down the Canadian Shield in nearby Algonquin Park.

I cried on the couch, face down, my youngest shaking me: "What's wrong, Mommy?"

My husband stormed around outside. He stepped through the door, said something loudly to me though I couldn't hear him; I moved to the bathroom. I crouched behind the shower curtain, knees pulled in tight, water pouring from my eyes. He moved to the doorway, not a step closer, told me I was being childish. All I could think is, *I need to leave, I need to leave, I need to leave.* I left, but there was nowhere to go. We were sanding the other down, flesh raw, rubbing up against open wounds.

We made sand that, as the wind blew, stung our eyes.

Everything was immediately better once the kids went back to school and we returned to our home, at a surface level. We found ourselves reunited in our joyful newfound freedom. But the stone that was carved away could not be put back to what it once was. The pandemic summer left us pocked with holes in places where love used to be.

If marriage is a sedimentary rock, it's important to consider that even a rock has a life cycle, and erosion is part of the process. With sedimentary rock, fragments of stone that break down get transported by the wind, water, and ice to somewhere new.[1]

But where did those pieces of us go? *I miss them.* And what were we becoming?

My husband and I used intimacy as a point of connection for a while, but something remained missing. Resentment, once it settles in, is a difficult stain to remove. The division of labour, with both of us home, continued to be a sore spot. Without travel, work office antics, date nights out, dinners in restaurants, live theatre, and weekend getaways, we had little to no time alone as a couple — little to no time alone for ourselves.

Books were a refuge. I happened across *How to Fall in Love with Anyone*, by Mandy Len Catron,[2] author of the viral *New York Times* "Modern Love" article[3] on the topic that features the author's own experiment with Arthur Aron's "36 Questions,"[4] a questionnaire designed to lead two participants to fall in love by asking the other person a series of increasingly intimate questions. Could completing the questionnaire infuse our union with an insurgence of fresh love?

On a Friday night close to Christmas, when my work was piling up more than usual and we both had a million things to do, I pulled out the love questionnaire.

"I know what we're doing tonight," I told him.

On our dog walk that morning, I had told him about Catron's book, sharing the anecdote that some people are cats — independent roamers — and some are dogs: loyal and attentive. The theory goes that two cats will get bored of one another and wander apart, while two dogs will smother each other. The perfect pair is a cat–dog mix. He lit up at the reference, having heard it on a Ricky Gervais podcast interview.

"What do you think we are?" I asked him.

"You're a cat and I'm a dog, obviously," he said, and I smiled in agreement.

Later that day, with the kids asleep, we settled on our plush sectional, the dog on the floor between us. I curled up with a bowl of popcorn and read out the first question.

"Given the choice of anyone in the world, whom would you want as a dinner guest?"[5]

My husband sat there deep in thought, furrowing his brow, looking off in the distance. He was taking the question of love seriously. I bit my lip to keep from smiling.

After fourteen years together, his answer surprised me.

"The prime minister of New Zealand," he declared, referring to Jacinda Ardern.

"What?" I was genuinely surprised. I assumed he'd pick one of the men he tends to read or listen to. "Why?"

"Because I think she would be interesting and a good role model for our girls to have around the table."

The dinner question effortlessly flushed out one of his most endearing qualities. Dan thinks of others and puts his family first. How had I somehow forgotten this about him? I felt an instant surge of love and affection, knowing he can still surprise me.

I opted to dine with writer and filmmaker David Shields, whom I admired for writing about the size of his penis. I thought he would make a great mentor and be interesting to talk to. My husband smiled at me, knowing I really did think that one day I would share a meal with Shields across the table. I made sure to remind him I had emailed Shields, recently, and complimented him on the penis description, the shock of the image having stayed with me and given me permission to write my own truth. Shields graciously responded, sharing an opportunity to work with him.

I am the cat, proudly carrying home dead birds that appeal only to me, and Dan is ever the devoted dog.

One method by which sedimentary rock is formed is from pieces of other existing rock.[6]

We took turns reading the questions, passing Catron's book back and forth. Dan surprised me again with question seventeen: "What is your most treasured memory?"[7]

"Trips to the convenience store with my grandma as a preteen," he said. "She let me pick an action movie and then we would watch it together."

Really? That was his most treasured memory? Who was this guy I married — some sort of saint?

Sedimentary rock is also formed from compressed organic material like plants, shells, and bones.[8]

These offerings from him were compacting down, building something new from something old and unusable. And I thought, maybe that was what love was, or what it was to be in a marriage. It's not that our love continues to grow, but that it breaks down after a time. Love cycles, and then renews itself again from what once was old.

Perhaps love is created by feeling seen.

To another question, I answered, "I am a serious person." In the truest sense of the term, I am not a serious person. I don't wear a suit, and nobody calls me "sir" or "madame." Dan compliments me on my ability to take a joke. "It's one of the things I like about you." But in another respect, I am wholly dedicated to my work as a disability-ally, my writing, and my family.

Dan looked at me solemnly. "You are a serious person. People wouldn't think that about you, maybe, because you're always smiling and super-friendly and nice, but you are. You're passionate."

We both paused. I saw myself in his blue-green eyes, and I felt naked, my core exposed. *I see you; you see me.*

With erosion, there is sediment, and once that sediment settles somewhere and enough of it accumulates, the lowest layers compact so tightly that they form solid rock. New rock is born.

And it was this act of being seen that compacted deep in my chest, expanding the size of my heart, which swelled with love.

For the final five questions, we moved to the intimacy of our bedroom. Every emotional need in my body was being met, each thread of intimacy knitted like organic material woven into something new. Reclining in bed, he propped his elbow up on his pillow, resting his cheek on his hand. We arrived at the last question as his eyes were drooping. We were nearing midnight, which for parents of three small children feels like four a.m.

"Share a personal problem and ask your partner's advice on how he or she might handle it. Also, ask your partner to reflect back to you how you seem to be feeling about the problem you have chosen."[9]

I said something cat-like. "What if I am bored with my partner and wanting a change?" What I really wanted to ask him was *what if my love ebbs and flows? What if the rock of our marriage is not as solid as society would have us believe?*

He responded with something dog-like — that I should consider whether that was really how I was feeling, because he didn't think it was. He then reflected back that I seemed to be "feeling silly" in regard to the problem I had chosen, and when he said "silly," his eyes bugged out, and he touched me in a way that made me laugh and our eyes met, and I remembered not to take myself so seriously. I saw into him and remembered that what we have is stable and solid, holes and all. And it was so because we chose for our love to be this way. We worked at it over time with questionnaires and open conversation. We rebuilt. When love struck, marriage was not an answer or a cure, it was the beginning of something new, a daily decision to love another person. Maybe loving another was allowing yourself and what was between you to erode away, be reshaped and remoulded with time, and to take new form, over and over again.

As suggested in Catron's book, following the questionnaire, we ended with four minutes of sustained gazing into each other's eyes, which was supposed to be a difficult and uncomfortable task. I nudged him to stay awake but decided not to do so again. By this point, we'd both gotten what we needed from the other.

But he stayed awake for me. As I looked into his eyes, I realized this was something I was comfortable with, something we had done many times before for many years; we'd loved and lingered in the eyes of the other. And even though something as diffuse and fluid as water can erode away something as hard and solid as rock over time, we easily made it to four minutes.

The next morning, we lay together, flesh and bones collided, compacting tightly into the other, and we made new love.

Extramarital Sex

IT'S LATE AT night, and my husband pulls out from inside of me and heads to the bathroom. I melt off the bed and follow behind him, slapping his naked ass on my way to the toilet as he bends over the sink, washing his face. He makes his way back to the bed and arrives under the sheets before me. I slide under the silky sheets too, positioning the length of our bodies side by side, and I prop my head up on my elbow, facing him. I nuzzle my face into his neck, inhaling the scent of our sex and his musk. The mix is intoxicating.

We spent the evening together, several hours of talking, which culminated in our lovemaking. I was away for six days for my MFA residency; we missed each other.

I told him about the closing lecture, "Why I Write," with *New Yorker* writer Adam Gopnik as a guest lecturer. He urged us to search for a "wild exactitude" in our writing. Gopnik shared a story of *New Yorker* writers who "couldn't spell and had bad grammar, but each one had a wild exactitude of his own." Gopnik talked about his friendship with Malcolm Gladwell, whom Dan admires, taking us to the scene of Gladwell's family dinner parties and relaying the story of Gopnik's son asking him if he knew it took ten thousand hours to become an expert — a phenomenon that Gladwell made famous.

"When did you start writing, Dad?"

Gopnik figured it was 1980. Then his son asked him about how many hours a day he wrote for, and Gopnik estimated four. His son did the math, taking into account a few holidays and some weekend downtime, and figured that meant it would take Gopnik about six years to get in his ten thousand hours and become an expert writer. Interestingly enough, Gopnik realized that his first *New Yorker* piece was accepted in 1986 — six years after he began writing. His friend Gladwell was right, that son of a gun. Gopnik pointed out that many professional programs are six years long: becoming a doctor, a lawyer, getting a Ph.D. He told me and my fellow classmates, "If you write for four hours a day for six years, you will be a professional writer."

I'm feeling like I've told a good story, but my husband's face — my husband who does have a Ph.D. that took him six years — says otherwise.

"That's horseshit! I don't like this guy," he says. "Two things. First of all, the math is all wrong. It would take more like ten years to become an expert at four hours a day, taking into account holidays and weekends. Second of all, those professionals he mentioned work way more than four hours a day. Lawyers article for eighteen-hour days — it's supposed to be one of the most gruelling experiences there is, and doctors are on call for twenty-four-hour days and work twelve-hour shifts. Also, the ten-thousand-hour thing is based on Anders Ericsson's research on deliberate practice."

"Okay, okay, but it was a nice story, wasn't it, with the son?" I insist. The writer in me holds on to the fantasy, swayed by the romantic notions that a perfect story sets into motion. In other words, it's easy to get swept up in a beautiful lie.

We switch gears, talk about my residency and New York City agent experience instead. An agent requested some of my material to read and I was ecstatic. Dan was right there with me, matching my enthusiasm over the phone, and now in person, he tells me, "I'm so proud of you, really." He tilts my chin up, looks me in the eyes.

We kiss.

"Thanks, it felt really nice — even if it doesn't go anywhere," I say.

"It isn't nice," he says, "it's *earned*; you worked hard to earn this, and you deserve it."

I ask him about his week, and he tells me about this show he's been watching, *Minions of Midas*, and a scene with a funny translation from Spanish to English he saw closed-captioned on the screen. "A mother and her adult daughter are talking," he explains, "and there's some attractive guy or something that's distracting the daughter at work, so she doesn't want to go in. The mother responds with: 'What — you don't trust your own pussy?'"

It might be the pussy comment that leads us to sex. We make love. Then the realigning of our bodies side by side, settling back into each other's arms. I'm wrestling with a question in my mind. I'm feeling a bit shy about the question because I know I shouldn't ask it. It's getting late; we should probably just go to sleep.

This fantastical question exists outside the realm of our relationship's boundaries. *Current* boundaries, I should say.

What happens when fantasy and reality collide?

That's not the question.

"Let's say," I ease into this, "hypothetically, totally hypothetically speaking, I wanted to have sex with another person. What would you say?"

"No," he wastes no time in answering.

"But wait, what about …"

"No. Definitely not," he says, then, joking, "What? You get interest from a New York agent and suddenly you're too good for me now?"

We both laugh.

"No, no! Hear me out, it's not like that."

We go back and forth for a while, me reiterating some version of the same question, him standing firm, resolute on the meaning of our marriage vows. He explains that our sex life is a pillar of our marriage and that if I were to have sex with someone else, it would not only topple the pillar of our marriage but also make him feel like he was a bad husband who couldn't satisfy his wife, so she had to go elsewhere.

"Being a good husband is an important part of my identity and so it would crumble my identity too."

"Okay, I can understand that." I sense a tiny desperation in his voice, a plea almost. *Stop.* But I keep going because he hasn't said what I want to hear. To clarify: I don't know what I want to hear, but I'll know it when I hear it (which also sounds like a line from a New York literary agent).

Three seconds later: "But what if we had never gotten married and just stayed together as life partners — then?"

"But we didn't do that — and no," he says.

"Why not?" I genuinely want to know.

"Because when I married you, that wasn't the deal. You committed yourself to me and I'm committed to you." He wraps his arm around me, squeezing me tight to his body momentarily. "You're locked in."

"Is this marriage a prison?" I'm playful and he's cooling down.

He settles onto his back.

I rub my hand up and down his bare leg. "Okay — but hold on a second. Would you be open to discussing —"

He cuts me off. "No. This is not an open marriage. I did not sign up for an open marriage — it's not what we agreed to." He moves away, so that my hand falls off his leg.

"Oh, don't be like that," I say.

"Are you asking for my permission? Because if you are, I'm saying no," he says.

"I don't need your permission for anything," I remind him.

"I know you don't, so then why are you asking?"

"Good point."

I don't let it go. I'm digging for something, I'm not sure what. Perhaps a pile of dirt in the face?

"Let me give you a scenario," I tell him. "I think that might help. Let's say it's a celebrity or someone I'm really attracted to."

I describe the poet Ross Gay, whose *Book of Delights* I've been reading. The man is tall, long fingers, strong hands, with a gorgeous smile, white teeth. When he gives a reading (I've watched his YouTube videos), he sways and bops to his own beat in a way that manages to be both endearing and sexy. After reading his work and watching his readings, I'm a little bit in love with him. How can you not be? But I have to confess, this isn't that surprising, considering I fall a little bit in love with people often, especially extraordinary people — before losing interest.

"Let's say I go away for a weekend and meet Ross Gay and he is interested in me. Let's say I have the opportunity to have a one-night stand with Ross Gay."

"Ross Gay!" Dan interrupts. "Nobody even knows who he is!"

I'm not deterred. "He was on *Oprah*, I think ... Anyway, it doesn't matter — I think he's sexy."

My husband is brooding beside me on the bed now. He's lying on his back, arms crossed, eyebrows furrowed. This conversation isn't going the way I planned — or rather, I have planned this conversation badly.

"You're upset?" I ask him.

"Of course I'm upset! How would you feel if I asked you that? What would your answer be? Is it okay if *I* have sex with another woman?"

"Obviously, no," I say, "but you don't *want* to have sex with anybody else — do you? I know you don't, but what if I do?"

"Then too bad, you're married to me," he says.

"But what if you didn't know?" I ask.

"Well, that would be your decision then, I guess," he says.

It would be? "Do you mean …"

"No. I mean, if you choose to make that decision and not tell me about it, there's nothing I can do."

I sit with that for a minute.

"Well, that would never work," I concede, "because I would only do it if you were okay with it."

"I already answered that question ten times." He's getting angry now.

This fantastical thinking has proven to be dangerous.

"Okay, okay, hold on. Let me explain. Let me explain."

"No. You don't need to explain anything. To me this is a black-and-white issue. You're being silly about this, and I don't like it or want to talk about it anymore."

I'm taken aback by his closed-mindedness in one respect, but on the other hand, this is the man I married. True to his values, devoted to his wife, and not into sharing her any more than I am into sharing him.

"But I'm a cat …" I say it pitifully. "Cats wander." I've lost him. "And I'm not being silly, I mean it. What if I wanted to have sex with someone else? Marriage lasts until the end of our lives. What if having sex with someone else was something I really wanted? Would you give that to me?"

"No."

"What about if I never told you? If when I went somewhere, if I met someone and we had sex, but I didn't tell you about it?"

"Well, like I said, then that would be your decision," he says, "and then it would also be my decision to not be in a marriage like that."

"But you wouldn't have to know …"

That would never work, he explains, because he would be thinking about it every time I went away and it would crack the foundation of our marriage anyway. I can't fault his logic.

He isn't looking at me anymore.

"I've hurt you. I'm sorry, babe. That wasn't my intention. Come here." I reach for his arms to try and uncross them, wiggle myself in.

He's reluctant.

"I love you," I tell him.

We've had many honest conversations with one another, but this one has pushed too far, breached a barrier of trust.

"I love you too, and I don't want to talk about this anymore, okay? Can we please go to bed?"

"As long as you're not mad at me."

He gives me a forceful kiss on the lips, meant to push me away. "Good night," and he turns away from me.

I'm left wondering why I felt the need to ask. Did I ask just for kicks (that seems cruel) or was it to define his limits? Was I trying to coax free his love for me, make it rise to the surface, that which is buried beneath the rigours of our daily lives? To bring the fantasy of my dreams into the everyday? Because I've been wanting sex? Because he gave me sex and I want more? Because I always want more? Because I'm insatiable? Because we've been married eleven years and I've been having sex with the same man for thirteen years? (*How will I feel at fifty years?*) Because variety is the spice of life? Because I'm bored (*am I bored?*), because I want to know if there's anything he won't do for me — even the unimaginable to most monogamous couples? Is it because I don't want to be like most couples? Because I see myself as a cat, a wanderer, interested in new experiences? Is it because I'm not sure I ever should have gotten married, and have spent time contemplating how that is the main narrative we are served up as little girls, the promise and pursuit of marriage, and how we choke the marriage rhetoric down like a disgusting medicine that's meant to make us feel better, to cure our ailment, remedy our delicate situation — that of being female? Do I just want to change things up? Or was the question asked to see how much he really loves me? *Does* he really love me? *How much* does he love me?

Am I worth fighting for?

I curl into him, the big spoon, wrapping my arms around him, and kiss him on the shoulders and back until we both fall asleep.

We sleep long and deep until the morning sun, jubilant, is calling through our bedroom curtains. I roll back to my husband's side and nuzzle into him. We slept with our backs to each other, in our own space, as usual. Two bodies, two hearts, in one bed. I press my fingers into his flesh, lower down. He's awake.

Before he says anything, I intuit what happened the night before has not been forgotten.

"Are you still mad at me?" I ask. "I'm sorry if I hurt your feelings last night."

He's looking at me through squinty, sleepy eyes.

"You did hurt my feelings," he accuses, "but it's okay."

Maybe that was what I wanted. To hurt his feelings. The perverse: pain is love.

"I'm sorry," I offer. And then I look directly into his eyes and whisper, "You mean everything to me."

That, I can attest, is my version of a wild exactitude. Marriage is wild; it is also precise in its meaning, its act of utter devotion. "The wildness is the drama," Gopnik said, and also, to paraphrase, "Write not just the pious march of statements the reader would agree with."

Dan kisses my lips, and we somehow manage to stay that way for hours, despite dog and children, without interruption — we kiss and fall into one another like every fantasy I've ever had. But real.

CHILD

Pins & Pine Needles

I'M LYING ON my stomach on our dock, looking down over the edge at a sheet of ice. The sun warms my back, but a frigid wind whips my face, tangles the loose strands of hair under my wool winter hat. Just yesterday, the lake was mostly melted, but I woke up this morning to a windswept block of ice and temperatures of ten degrees below zero. I had the foresight to fill most of our water buckets beforehand, thankfully. I feel cradled by the wooden boards below me and the sun above, which offers its warmth, but all the while the wind claws at my face, rips at my clothing. Life is constantly like this: two extremes, comfort and pain, each pulling in opposite directions. At the moment, I feel the sting of the wind keenly. I'm just back from an outing with the girls and the dog, where I was the only adult on hand. Things did not go as planned.

You know when you're doing the best you can, and someone criticizes you for it?

We are staying in our cottage, which is designed for balmier climates. The cold seeps in and we blast our heaters. Dan has an all-afternoon meeting and so I plan to take the girls and dog for a trail walk at Algonquin Park. The forty-five-minute drive there, our boardwalk hike, and the drive back will give him some reprieve. I owe him that much; he's been looking after our family lately.

✳

We arrive at the trail and — to my dismay — the ice visibly coats our pathway. I chose the one-and-a-half-kilometre boardwalk trail because I hoped that, like on our dock, the ice would be melted away. I was optimistic that once we began walking, we'd find the ice melted in patches. I knew there was no way Elyse would walk on the icy path, but we'd come all this way.

"Come on, kiddo!" I say. "Let's go."

Ariel stands at the mouth of the trail with her hand outstretched. She reaches for chickadees, calling to them like I taught her. Penelope observes. Elyse stands in the parking lot, holding her hood up over her ears as the wind howls.

"No!" she says. "Car!"

I haven't even introduced the dog into the equation yet.

Louie comes bounding out of his crate from the trunk and runs past the two girls onto the trail, scattering the birds and a handful of red squirrels, which chitter off. He is enthralled. The wilderness is his element. He loves to run ahead of our pack and has good recall. *Good*, not perfect. He's a specimen of a dog to behold.

"I got honked at today!" Dan told me after a run earlier in the month.

"Oh yah, way to go," I said.

"Yah, a guy slowed down and yelled out his window that he had a Vizsla too and Louie was a good-looking boy."

I take note of the three other cars in the trailhead parking lot and think, *Okay, maybe we won't run into anyone.* I keep Louie on a long leash so I can step on it or grab it if I have to. He's a friendly dog, with rambunctious, slightly anxious tendencies. I'd rather we didn't run into anyone.

Elyse has made it clear she's not budging, so I do the thing I said I'd never do again. "Do you want a piggyback ride?"

In retrospect, I will think of this walk in terms of possibilities. It is *possible* that Elyse may give my arms and back a break, and that she will walk some of the one and a half kilometres and help me out instead of demanding to be carried. It's *possible* that we won't run into anyone and that my dog will behave. It's *possible* that the walk will be enjoyable, that my responsibilities will not weigh on me like a burden. It's *possible*. At the beginning, the hike is full of possibility. Keeping my dog under control and my children happy is not an impossible task, after all, though sometimes it feels that way.

The ice is unabating, ever present. We come to one of the spruce bogs, the trail's namesake, a section of path that is open, unsheltered by trees. And while I am captivated by the beauty of the pine backdrop and wide, rapidly flowing stream beneath us, the wicked wind is tearing through the corridor and Elyse is screaming bloody murder in my ears. My arms struggle to hold her up. And just ahead, I make out three figures. I call Louie back to me and he comes. Without the use of my arms, I step on his leash and halt him in his tracks — momentarily. He breaks free and runs back up ahead to greet the passersby, and decides to bark at the third person the moment I step on his leash again. I apologize and move past them, no harm done. Elyse still tethered to my back, all forty-five pounds of her, I press on. I decide that if Louie is going to bark, for the next group we see I will set Elyse down and make Louie sit patiently while they pass. That way, I won't be in the wrong. I envision this course of action as the right one to take, a pleasant possibility to hold on to in case I need it.

Elyse continues her refusal to walk. I choose each step along the slick path deliberately, carefully. I can't afford to fall and take us both down. Penelope, four years old, slips onto her backside twice.

"I'm okay!" she says both times, jumping back up to her feet, skating ahead. Our troupe presses on.

I see two more figures approaching in the distance.

"Louie! Come." I duck behind a tree and slide Elyse off my back. This move of hide-and-go-seek is irresistible to my dog. Louie has to come find me. His refusal to do so is an impossibility.

He comes.

I grab his leash. Make him sit. I brandish a treat in front of his nose, hold his gaze. "Good boy." And the three of us wait. I call ahead to the other two, "Just stay there!" They wait. We are five frozen statues in a corridor of pines. Later, I see five white pines, tall, proud, and twisted, and I think *that's us*. The two young women take their time making their way past. Louie holds position; I'm standing on his leash, holding Elyse's hand. Waiting. I don't mind waiting. Waiting is something I'm used to doing. Okay — I do mind. But waiting is for the best.

As the young woman passes me, I catch her eye.

I say something friendly to her, a throwaway comment like, "Just trying to keep everybody wrangled," or something like that. Her response could be anything else, something different. A million different options. But she chooses a dagger.

"Well, maybe it would be easier to rein everybody in if you kept your dog on his leash. It *is* the rules, you know." And she gives me a knowing look. A look that says, "I am following the rules and you are not and I am so much better than you because of it."

I say nothing, just purse my lips. I have my foot on my dog's leash. He sits there, doing nothing wrong.

She is right, of course. But also wrong.

Inside, I am fuming. *I am doing the best I can; can't she see I am doing the best I can?*

She doesn't care. That young woman didn't see a mom struggling to keep her three kids and dog safe and happy. She didn't see me walking gingerly across the ice path, one kid with Down syndrome balanced on my back. She saw her opportunity at self-righteousness, and she took it. *Somebody please crown her head, break out the applause.* And so the heat inside me rises and my ability to ignore her words subsides. She has handed me an unkindness, made it impossible to ignore my feelings of failure. Who can succeed when they feel judged?

And from there, the walk unravels. Elyse clamours back onto me and cries when the wind bites at her face again. My arms ache. Louie chases two Canada geese as we approach the highway and I struggle to control him.

A hundred metres from the parking lot, I leave the girls stranded, an island unto themselves, and run ahead to put Louie in the car. *How dare that woman say that to me? How thoughtless. Can't she see I'm doing my best?* And *How dare Elyse insist I carry her the whole way?* My arms are shaking from the exertion, the frustration and exhaustion.

By the time I get everyone back in the car, I feel the wall erect inside me, made of hot rage. The sensation is like pins and needles, the contradiction of hot and cold. I feel numb. I'm like the lake at our cottage, free flowing one minute, then turned by a chilling wind into a solid block of ice.

That wasn't at all what I wanted, I think. Does it matter, what I want? And it is in these moments that the impossibility of my life fills me. I cannot take care of my dog and my children on my own, I think. *It's impossible.*

With Louie, Elyse, and Penelope safely secure in the car, I join Ariel back at the entrance of the trail and hold my hand outstretched. Maybe the birds will comfort me. One chickadee alights on my hand as though it were a branch, and then another. In the car driving, I will think about this, how it is possible that I can hold a winged creature, wildness itself, in the palm of my hand — a seemingly impossible feat when you envision a free bird soaring high in the clouds — but I can't go for a walk with my kids and dog, my daily companions, without feeling like a complete failure.

On the drive home, I turn the music up and think about contradictions in life: how we make our decisions hoping they will lead to happiness, but there is no recourse when they don't. You can't put the children back where they came from, or rehome the dog you've tamed for acting the way you've tamed him. And I don't want the things I love to go away, either — that would be the worst idea. A true impossibility to my heart. I just don't want everything to feel so damn hard all the time, or the confusion of contradictions to barrage my brain. *Comfort and pain, each pulling in opposite directions.*

Back in town, about five minutes from our cottage, the name of a church I've never noticed before jumps out at me. The sign reads "The Church of Epiphany." Is this supposed to be emblematic? A first-of-the-month April Fool's joke? What is the epiphany here? Where is my moment of great realization?

I send the children inside the cottage and make my way down to the frozen lake.

I'm lying belly down, looking at the ice from the edge of our dock. The cold wind remains savage, but it's possible I don't mind. I see something out of the corner of my eye. The ice is thick, complete, yet creeping toward me is a thin layer of water. *Hope*, I think, though my mind rallies against it. What feels impossible becomes possible, with hope, I concede. Tiny miracles. Water that resists freezing, resists its own nature.

The Mushroom

WORKING TOGETHER, TREES and fungi may live for many hundreds of years. The two are co-dependent, one offering what the other does not have. The trees provide their sugar as sustenance and their carbon, which fungi convert and store in the soil. The fungi offer the trees life-sustaining minerals and extend the reach of the tree's roots, allowing them to take in more water.[1]

Trees also need to communicate and swap nutrients with one another, and they do so through an underground fungal network known as the "mycelium." The mycelium is a mass of threads with trillions of end branches that functions similarly to the neural pathways in our brains. Trees send chemical compounds and electrical impulses through the fungi, a flowing underground root river. When trees grow together, connected by the mycelium, nutrients and water can be optimally divided between them so that each tree can grow to be its best self. The stronger trees share their resources with the weaker trees, and when the strong become sick, they are in turn looked after by the weaker trees. Trees understand that every tree suffers when we look out only for ourselves, and every tree is

valuable to the community. A tree can be only as strong as the forest that surrounds it.[2]

Trees depend on fungal networks, the mycelium, to survive, and
the mycelium's flower is the mushroom.

❋

I walk my dog at the cottage to the top of the gravel driveway, where
it's flat. I'm meandering, thinking about my day, while rust-coloured
seven-month-old Louie tears around up ahead of me, then drops
behind, nose to the ground. I pivot at the top of the long drive, as
I usually do, and in the next step, the next breath, I catch sight of
a magnificent mushroom. Its top reminds me of a frisbee, flat and
round. I marvel at its creation, its size, and the very fact of its being.

Snap. In an instant, the mushroom I'm admiring is destroyed,
its life incidentally obliterated by my Vizsla, who glided right on
by me and, with one careless step, toppled the formidable fungus,
leaving its fragile stem snapped at the base. Am I meant to feel
something? What does the mushroom's demise mean? My immediate gut reaction is one of partial regret and wonder: partial in that
I am not overly attached to this mushroom, and regret because the
mushroom will now cease to grow owing to the chance encounter
with my dog and I stumbling into its path. I wonder at my own ...
is it anger? Disappointment? I feel conflicted emotion at the mushroom for not defending itself better. *Now why would you go and
grow a flimsy neck like that when you have such a big head?* I blame
the victim. The mushroom was brave enough to grow in the heart
of the driveway, but why would it do such a thing? Why didn't it
hide, protect itself better? It's a wonder a toadstool can survive at all
with wild animals stalking about, taking a simple stroll and cutting
them down with the graze of bare knees.

I'm angry at the mushroom, but am I not also angry at myself for being part of the destruction? For being vulnerable in and of my own right? At realizing that I, too, hold a large and heavy head atop a flimsy neck, and that one day, it could snap. Or is it my maternal instincts kicking in, grieving the loss of a life in the way only a mother who has created and nurtured it can?

What a delicate life the fungi lead — are we so different?

✳

For fungi to be become attached to the tree's soft root hairs, the tree must be receptive. One and a half million species of fungi exist — four to six times more than plant species — and there are over sixty thousand varieties of trees on our planet.[3] Mycelium partnerships are tree-specific, which is to say that fungi partner only with specific trees; the relationship between the two is a delicate balance.

✳

That night, at bedtime, I'm in charge and all hell breaks loose. I promise a story as a bribe to the first girl in bed. Penelope is writhing on the floor. Elyse is upset and Ariel lies patiently in bed, silently praising herself for being first, because I have lost the energy and will to do so. We are on month 5,008 or thereabouts of the global pandemic, everyone home, and parental patience is wearing thin. "Translucent" may be a better word.

✳

Fungal connections come with a price to the trees. Without food, fungi would starve, so they exact payment from their partner trees in the form of carbohydrates. Fungi demand up to a third of the tree's total food production in return for their services. In exchange for their sugary reward, fungi filter out heavy metals, which are less harmful to the fungi than to the tree's roots and provide medical services by warding off intruders, including attacks by insects, bacteria, or fellow fungi.[4]

※

I lie on my stomach on top of my eldest daughter's quilt, and she requests a continuation of a story I told her a month ago, about a sabre-toothed tiger. I can barely remember what I had for dinner, let alone a tiger story I made up more than a month ago, so instead I describe a bland version of real life and kids going back to school.

Ariel reaches up and presses my cheeks with both hands. "Bad story," she complains.

"Don't touch my face, please." I am not in the mood, and my impatience rises to the surface.

I move to the next room, where Elyse is audibly complaining about I-have-no-idea-what and Penelope is crying for her story.

"I wanted to be first!"

"But you'll get the end story, the last story," I promise her. "The last story's better. I'll make it the best one."

"Heeeey!" Ariel complains from the other room.

I sit on the edge of Penelope's bed and look at Elyse. She's slumped on her bed, limp, like a tired dandelion in her yellow pyjama top.

"Do you want a snuggle?" I ask her.

"Yeah." To my surprise, she agrees. She's a big-time daddy's girl, especially at bedtime.

I gather her up in my arms — like Kim Fahner's line of poetry I read earlier in the day: *Gather me in now / for my heart is lost*[5] — and she rests her chin on my shoulder. Elyse is seven, nearly eight, but as she's done since she was an infant, her eyelids droop and she falls asleep in my arms. She relaxes into me and then she's gone, fast asleep. Something about her fragility then, her dependence on me as her mother, reminds me of the mushroom — the one we killed. Is it that having Down syndrome sets her apart, like that lone spindly stalk? Set apart and at risk. Set apart and at risk of being kicked, toppled over.

Why is it that I shy away from vulnerability, that anger rose inside me when the mushroom toppled over, that I need my kids to be tougher? I allow myself moments of vulnerability — in my writing, to be sure — but do I allow others the same courtesy? I have a hard time accepting vulnerability in other people, especially those I love. Is this some form of protection, some method of self-preservation? A shield I've forged around myself. *Bad things wouldn't have happened to you*, I'd tell them, *if you'd planned ahead, picked a better patch of grass, changed the way you're grown.* And that's it, isn't it. That Elyse can't change the way she was grown. She was born in the middle of the path with a big head and flimsy stalk. She's at risk. Physicians and pregnant parents like me used that word — and frequently still do — to talk about Down syndrome. *The risk* of carrying a fetus with Down syndrome. A risk to what or to whom? I wasn't sure in pregnancy, but now I see the risk is the other way around. My daughter is the one who is constantly put in harm's way by society's perceptions of the value of her life.

We are reluctant to see the potential and contributions of people with Down syndrome. *Grow tall, little mushroom*, we tell her. *You can even go to school alongside the other toadstools*, we promise her. *But once you grow big and strong, you do not belong in the workforce; out in the community, there will be nowhere for you to go, not with your flimsy neck and big head, so we will leave you, out in the open, exposed and detached. And life will trample you down.*

And life will trample you down.

As her mother, I am there to bear witness to her pain, as I witnessed the mushroom knocked carelessly to the ground.

But there's something else. Something more.

A tree can be only as strong as the forest that surrounds it.

I am the tree and she is my toadstool. We depend on one another. We are grown from the same soil; we just happen to differ by the count of our chromosomes. But like the trees and the toadstools, we need each other. What my daughter has to offer is unique to her in all the world.

Fungi are their own kingdom altogether. And human beings, as animals, are more closely related to fungi than to any other kingdom.[6]

At my worst, I blame my children for the way they are made, for the way my husband and I have made them, and the way they have become. *Bad things wouldn't have happened to you* … if you had slowed down instead of running, you wouldn't have tripped and scraped your knee; if you had washed your hands, you wouldn't have gotten sick from handling toads; if you'd eaten your vegetables and brushed your teeth, you wouldn't have gotten that cavity; if you'd just been kind, you wouldn't have gotten into that fight with your sister.

Bad things wouldn't have happened to you if you had never been born with Down syndrome. Sometimes I feel this way. At my worst. Sometimes. But all these comments I might make in distress — *now why would you go and grow a flimsy neck like that when you have such a big head?* — have more to do with my issues, my neurosis as a mother, than they ever have to do with the children's actions and behaviours themselves. They certainly didn't want to fall and scrape their knee; they certainly didn't intend the damage, but when the damage is done, I fault them because it is my job to keep them safe, and in a self-aggrandizing way, they have prevented me from doing so by virtue of their being. But I brought them here, I called their spirits forth, and so I am responsible for them, and I do not like to fail. I do not like to see my children injured and so I … injure them further? I'm not proud of my ability to chastise the broken, the already downtrodden; to embody the weakness I despise.

🜚

Four and a half billion years ago, fungi climbed out of the sea, became land pioneers, and brought life to earth. Fungi carry the wisdom of a billion years. Notably, through every major extinction event, the organisms that paired themselves with fungi survived.[7]

🜚

As a small child, I understood life, my life, to be permanent. Eternal existence. Is it the realization of my own vulnerability that causes me to feel empathy for the mushroom? Yes.

And sometimes, my daughter having Down syndrome is enough. I do not need one more thing to worry about, not one more mushroom to fall.

🜚

I lower Elyse, my little toadstool, gently from my embrace back onto her bed, and she lands like a bag of bones. She stirs, but her arms remain raised, half-bent above her head, almost as though she is throwing them up in prayer or devotion. She is as peaceful as peaceful can be, and I am happy to have given her what she needs. She is tiny, no big head at all. And while she is physically flimsy at first glance, her slumbering spirit is strong. She is alive and worthy — as worthy as I'll ever be as her mother.

⁕

We divided from fungi 650 million years ago. They remain inside of us. "We are the descendants of mycelium," says mycologist Paul Stamets in the documentary *Fantastic Fungi*. "Mycelium is the mother of us all."

⁕

A month later, I walk back to that same spot at the top of the hill with my dog and leave without finding even a trace of the large mushroom, as though it has never existed. But then, how could it have become so important to me? All is not lost. In its stead, I find clusters of tiny mushrooms, earth-toned and thriving, and I can't help but wonder if this is how life gets packaged up and re-parcelled. Nothing goes to waste. Everything and everyone serves a purpose. Something new has sprouted in the place of what was there before. "We are not an individual," says Stamets. "We are a vast network of molecules and energy wavelengths. The inter-connectedness of being is who we are."[8]

Now I am grateful for the mushrooms, mindful of them. I am extra careful where I step.

The Giving Tree

Before it dies, a Douglas-fir, half a millennium old,
will send its storehouse of chemicals back down into
its roots and out through its fungal partners, donating
its riches to the community pool in a last will and testament. We might well call these ancient benefactors
Giving Trees.[1]

— *The Overstory*, by Richard Powers

MY NEPHEW ROWAN'S birthday is in early June, when the
spring flowers of my in-laws' replete gardens bloom and appear
in their full resplendence. I crack open the hard cover of the
book Dan and I have gifted him — Shel Silverstein's *The Giving
Tree*[2] — to the first page. Dan and I are in the spring of our ro-
mance — babies, really. I feel a need to perform in front of his
older sister and parents, to impress upon them that I will one day
be a fantastic teacher. Look how well I read! And that I will also
be an amazing mother and wife. Look how generous I am with

my time! Look at how I adore children and hold their attention! When the actual time comes, there will be no doubt about my superior skills.

I open my reading with verve and zeal.

"And the boy loved the tree ... very much. And the tree was happy."[3] Overexaggerated smile.

Undoubtedly, my young nephew was paying close attention.

✳

At some point, the enthusiasm in my voice might have faded. You can't help but let melancholy seep in when you read *The Giving Tree*. The boy takes what he wants and leaves the tree, who loves him, behind. The tree isn't happy until she's given everything of herself, absolutely everything, to the boy. And the boy isn't happy until he's taken away every part of the tree.

Where's the joy in that?

"And so the boy cut down her trunk and made a boat and sailed away. And the tree was happy ... but not really."[4]

Reading the book then, I felt a sense of indignation on behalf of the tree. Why did the boy have to be so greedy as to take it all? The tree gives everything to the boy — and for what?

It is only at the beginning of his life and nearing its end that the boy is able to appreciate the tree for her true worth: for what she is instead of what she can provide. I'm reminded of a line from Haruki Murakami's memoir, *What I Talk About When I Talk About Running*: "I don't think we should judge the value of our lives by how efficient they are."[5] The same could be said for trees, and for humans.

I'm not sure whether my nephew hung on to my every word. I can't even picture where the two of us were sitting, as the Earth outside renewed itself around us. Was he snuggled into me on the couch or sitting in the armchair across from me? Was I in the armchair and he on the couch? The specifics don't matter. What was important was that when I finished reading that book, I knew one thing: I never wanted to be the tree.

＊

More than ten years later, the school day is nearly done. I tuck three mini boxes of Smarties into my coat pocket to dole out, one for each girl. I greet you with a kiss on the forehead and take your backpack from you. You hand it to me today, which is nice. Sometimes you leave it for me on the ground. Often you throw it on the ground. The wind feels rough, bitter cold. Winter whispers her frosty breath. You refuse to wear a hat or put your hood up or wear gloves. Your hands are bright pink, but you don't seem to mind. We're on our way home and it's just another day. The Smarties will keep you happy for a while.

We walk in a small cluster: me, you, your older and younger sisters. Your hands slide inside the too-long sleeves of your jacket and I hold loosely onto your sleeve in an attempt to keep our cluster moving, to keep you happy. And you are fairly happy. *Smarties!* This makes you smile and so I am smiling.

You say something, something I can't understand. I ask you to repeat, but I can't quite catch the meaning.

We approach Charlie, your favourite crossing guard, and you find your place by his side, take his hand, and we safely cross the street.

I offer to take back the now-empty Smarties box.

"Yes." You hand me the miniature cardboard container.

I think this is all you need. I hope.

But on the other side of the crosswalk, you ask again for something. Again, I do not understand you. Softly, I ask you to please repeat, but I don't stop walking, I press on. I sense things are moving in the wrong direction and, when this happens, I just want us to be home.

You don't try to explain again. You won't; instead, you start to scream. "No! No! No!"

"Honey, honey, what's wrong?" I ask, even though I know it's because I haven't understood you. Once we've reached tears, we have moved beyond solving what is wrong.

Frustration prevents words and what comes out are wails and screams.

This happens so fast, this transition from walking along the sidewalk together, smiling and eating Smarties, to you screaming and wailing, and I just want it to stop.

"Stop, Lysie!" your little sister yells at you.

Your big sister walks apart from us, way far ahead.

On the surface I remain kind, perplexed, even with the feeling of sinking dread settling in. This is an all-too-familiar scenario.

The thing you tried to say: what was it?

I stop walking now and face you. Crouch down to your level. What else is there to do?

"Are you cold? Are your hands cold? Here." I pull up your hood and you wail louder.

I plead with you for a while. "Please, Elyse, stop screaming. What's wrong?"

But the words are drowned out by a flood of tears.

I change my strategy, pick up my pace. We live only five hundred metres from the school.

"Come on, Elyse, let's go home. It's cold outside. We can talk at home."

I avoid the words I usually say in this scenario: "Daddy's at home. Let's go see Daddy." Daddy is always the prize. Daddy gets to be the prize and I feel like the problem. He tells me she does the same thing to him, in reverse, but I think he is only trying to be nice.

I don't ask if you're hungry either. I won't consider it now. I'm done with stopping a hundred metres from home and opening containers in the freezing cold. You can wait. Why can't you just wait? If that's what it is.

Your throat becomes unblocked long enough to say you'd like more Smarties, and now I'm annoyed, because these tears, this outrage, this emotional upset *for what?* A few more coloured pieces of chocolate?

I pick up my pace. "Come on, Elyse!" I wonder what my neighbours must think to see my daughter with Down syndrome wailing frequently as she walks down the street with me. They must think I'm a horrible mother, that something is terribly wrong. That I have hurt her, in some way. These thoughts make me feel guilty of a crime I don't understand or didn't commit. Mothers are forever getting it wrong.

When I move away from you, closer toward home, as a tactic to get you to keep moving forward, you only wail louder, and so I stop. You catch up. At one point you hit me. Your delicate blows are like wayward branches hitting the windowpane in a breeze, more an annoyance, the worry of scratched glass. You lack the physical power of the wind, but you make up for it with a storm of emotion. Your storm is like a heaving black cloud that's burst, and even though I know it's coming, there's no time to take cover before I'm soaked through.

I am swatted for my misunderstanding, for my lack of understanding, of being understood. Have I done this to you before? Your tears claw at my insides.

I think you are yelling at me for more Smarties, and finally, I've had enough.

"That is *enough*, Elyse. Cut it out — cut that out. Let's get home."

Somehow, using a firm voice, I have regained the upper hand, but now I feel terrible. I have regained control by silencing you.

Your face is red now, from the wind and your tears. A thin trail of clear fluid drains from your left nostril. I move in silence the rest of the way home, angry at you for making me the bad parent, yet again. Yet again, another day, another ordinary day, when I have walked you home in tears. Tears that seem to come and fall on a whim. Tears to which I can attach no meaning. And this hurts my feelings. Mothers have feelings too, you know. This hurts my feelings until I am the one who wants to cry, who should be crying. Who later will cry, alone in bed.

I try to understand you, but I feel like you don't try to understand me. I don't trust you. I don't trust that you won't burst into tears for reasons I can't explain and make me look like a bad mom who doesn't get her kid. And that is the source of my frustration: being humiliated by my own incompetence.

When you were in kindergarten and I picked you up at the end of the day, pushing a stroller with your then baby sister in it, you would throw your bag to the ground at my feet and wail from tiredness or hunger or just because you could or, most likely, because of some reason unknown to me, and other parents would turn to me, visibly disturbed, because this was obviously the most upsetting for *them*, and they would ask me, "What's wrong?" What they really meant to ask was, *how can we make her stop?* Other times their generosity was too much, *what can I do*, their eyes pleaded. *Nothing — stop looking at the spectacle of us; please go away.* But I didn't really mean that. Not that I wanted to be a spectacle — I didn't; but that I can do it alone — I can't.

Sometimes I want to be like the French photographer Anna Grevenitis. Her photography appeared in the *New Yorker*, an evocative series of black-and-white photographs she took of herself and her daughter with Down syndrome, engaging in daily tasks together.[6] Anna, the mother, looks directly at the camera in each shot. In one photo, she holds out her foot for her daughter, who's painting her toenails while facing squarely into the lens in defiance, the tattoos and shaved head on her left side on full display.

When you are crying, I want to freeze-frame, shoot the camera, with just my steely gaze staring back at onlookers. I want to dare them, with cold eyes, to even look at me or you. Sometimes I just want to hide; I don't feel like picking up children from school and disturbing the positive flow of my afternoon. Children are such unknowns.

I'm trying, Elyse — I'm trying. Do you see me trying?

⚜

We burst through the door to our house and you're still wailing and now I'm anger boiling over, frustrated in my own right. Now I throw your backpack onto the floor.

Why do we have to do this. Every. Single. Day. Same old shit, and I'm tired of it.

Your backpack sits askew alongside the backpacks belonging to your sisters and I move past them into the kitchen to cool off. Your tears are subsiding, but I need to be away from you. I'm trying not to be angry at you for being upset, because that isn't fair. It isn't fair to be mad at someone who's hurt, but now I am hurt too, and whose feelings matter? Do a mother's feelings count at all?

I empty someone's lunch bag, perhaps pull the yogourt container out of the fridge for a snack. When I turn back around, you are sitting on the floor beside your backpack and fingering your "stick," a beloved fishing rod that belongs to a board game where fish get hooked onto the end. I had no idea the stick was tucked into your backpack. Nobody told me. Or so I thought.

You're holding the small rod in one hand and fondling the hook on the end of the string with the other, mesmerized. "My stick. My stick."

"Elyse," I say, "you wanted your stick?"

"Yah," you say.

"Okay, then, next time, instead of screaming and crying, can you please just say that. 'Mommy, I want my stick'?"

And you sit there, eyes focused on the hook, dangling, dangling. Swaying back and forth. You are calming yourself down with the hypnotizing motion.

And I think back to the walk and remember you said the word "stick." Right after we crossed the street with Charlie, right before the tears.

"I want my stick."

That might have been what you said.

I was carrying it the whole time in the backpack on my shoulders.

I would have given it to you, had I known; of course I would have given it to you.

"Sorry, Elyse. Mommy didn't know."

But I'm not feeling very sorry and my words come out indifferent, without affect. I'm still feeling angry, hurt, betrayed. *Sorry I didn't know about your stupid fucking stick.*

I feel angry, but that feeling oscillates with a sort of knowing empathy. I can't ignore the telepathy mothers intuit about their children's thoughts and emotions. You just wanted your stick, and nobody gave it to you. Your own mother wouldn't listen.

Why didn't I just stop moving for a minute more?

But it's not that simple. We have a past. I did stop moving, remember? And tears. More tears. Wails. A mother can only take so much.

I have two other children. A husband. A dog. Myself to worry about.

Ariel. She was gone. Long gone down the street. I was in no position to ask about her day. Other than telling you to stop, Penelope stayed silent. She's the one new to kindergarten, who should have been crying from exhaustion and hunger. The children have learned there's only room for one person's tears. It isn't always you, to be sure, but your tears stain me in a way that's hard to explain. I find it hard not to take your tears personally, when I have tried so hard. Perhaps it is the trying that's the problem.

From where I'm standing in the kitchen, I can hear the dog whining in his crate in the living room. I call your dad to come upstairs from the basement, away from his work.

"I need your help," I tell him. I can't take it, this not being good at my job.

He comes upstairs and finally I can breathe. The piano teacher arrives and you are smiling again. A deep exhale, and I'm getting there too. The piano teacher passes me a loaf of bread, freshly baked by her husband, a thank you for some editing work I did for him. A job I am good at. *Food!* Now I am happy again. I am like the giving tree. *But not really.*

✳

Later that night, in bed, I'm reading Richard Power's *The Overstory* and the idea of the giving tree reappears in a new form. "People see better what looks like them," he writes. "*Giving trees* is something any generous person can understand and love."[7]

✳

The next day, I try again. To be a good mother, that is.

I double down on my efforts. I grab three boxes of rainbow-coloured chocolatey orbs and one "stick," which I pocket.

The weather is fair today — no need for mittens. I arrive at the school and greet all three children with hugs and kisses. You pass me your backpack, gently.

"I'm going home," you say, heading off through the field that cuts to the sidewalk.

Fair enough.

When I catch up to you, I offer you Smarties.

"No," you say, "I want fruit snacks."

"Hmm, well, I don't have any fruit snacks with me, but let's check your lunch bag."

The fruit snack packet, which I cut open in the corner for you before school, is empty.

"Oh, you already ate your fruit snacks."

"No, no …" There's less conviction in your voice, some confusion, no rising hysteria. You simply look as perplexed as I am.

"Do you want your stick?" Ah, the art of distraction.

"Yes!"

And we're off walking again, both of us in a good mood, past Charlie, the crossing guard, to the other side of the street and the final stretch.

You giggle most of the way home. Perhaps I overexaggerated earlier. Perhaps you get your flair for the melodramatic from me.

I use a line pilfered from your father. "Hey chicken wing, chicken wing," and I nudge into your side with my chicken wing elbow. "How was your day, chicken wing?"

And you giggle this adorable laugh that's like the ringing of a bell, pure and true.

"No, no," you say through your giggles, "I want Daddy." You aren't laughing now, but you aren't upset, either.

I nudge you again, gently, in the ribs. "Your daddy doesn't want you." I use a fake evil voice.

And at this, you laugh and laugh at the ridiculous statement.

And then you play my game.

"Daddy doesn't want you!" you say.

"No, doesn't want you!" I counter.

"No, you!"

"No, you!"

And on this goes until your pure joy is written across my face in a warm, wide smile. I wish now that everyone in the world could see us together.

You curl your tiny fingers around my arm and we swing along that way, arm in arm, having found our common ground. Comedy. You are a comedian, after all.

When we get home, I unpack your lunch bag and there, at the bottom, are your fruit snacks, which have dumped out through the hole I cut in the package in the morning.

"Elyse, your fruit snacks are all here! I'm sorry, sweetheart." I beam at her. "And you didn't cry! Thank you for not crying, Elyse, when you didn't get what you wanted. I'm sorry I didn't see them."

I squeeze her little shoulders and she shrugs it off.

No big deal.

*

As I finish this essay, Penelope comes into the room, seeking my attention. I happen to be holding my own copy of Silverstein's *The Giving Tree* in my hands. I have been perusing its pages, considering the significance of the text.

"Can I have that book?" Penelope says, taking it from my grasp. She isn't really asking.

Another line from *The Overstory* is jogged from memory: "A tree is a wonderous thing that shelters, feeds, and protects all living things. It even offers shade to the axmen who destroy it."[8]

And so it is with children, who pare us down one limb at a time.

I smooth out the crown of curls on my four-year-old daughter's head as she sits cross-legged on the floor beside me, turning the pages and studying them intently.

"That was a short read," she says, handing it back to me.

And the tree was happy.

Reverberations of Institutional Violence: A Spectrum

This essay is dedicated to Bill, aka 'Boo', and to his sister, Dr. Catherine McKercher, author of *Shut Away: When Down Syndrome Was a Life Sentence.*[1]

TIME IS SUPERFLUOUS. The cries of yesteryear roar and echo into the present and past injustices overflow into today.

In their book, *Institutional Violence and Disability: Punishing Conditions*, Kate Rossiter and Jen Rinaldi explain that institutional violence occurs along a spectrum.

> At one end is "cold violence," or the dozens of large and small indignities of daily life on the inside ... At the other end of the spectrum is "hot violence" — rape and other sexual abuse, torture, and acts of sheer cruelty with the sole purpose of

gratifying the person inflicting the pain. It's the kind of violence that is likely to attract media attention or, in some cases, lead to criminal charges.[2]

1) I sat on the other side of a windowless room, looking through the glass of the two-way mirror at Elyse, who was getting quizzed on her letters of the alphabet. I noticed myself becoming agitated, but I stayed calm. Elyse seemed disinterested and gave half-hearted answers. By the time the session was over, I was indignant on behalf of my daughter.

"So, we're going to work on her letters," the therapist told me.

"No, you're not," I said. "Elyse knows her letters. She knows her letters in English and in French. She's known her letters since she was three years old. She knew her letters before her older sister. I do *not* want her working on the letters of the alphabet again."

2) The therapist was taken aback by my forwardness. On the drive home, I was livid. Why would a therapist assume a seven-year-old didn't know her letters?

Cold Violence[3]

Cold Violence is characterized by a denial of individual choice,
privacy and dignity,
and uses shame-inducing rituals.

A) Infantilized
The institutional violence of the past exists today.
Mind-numbing activities
The intergenerational trauma
of abuse
gets handed down.

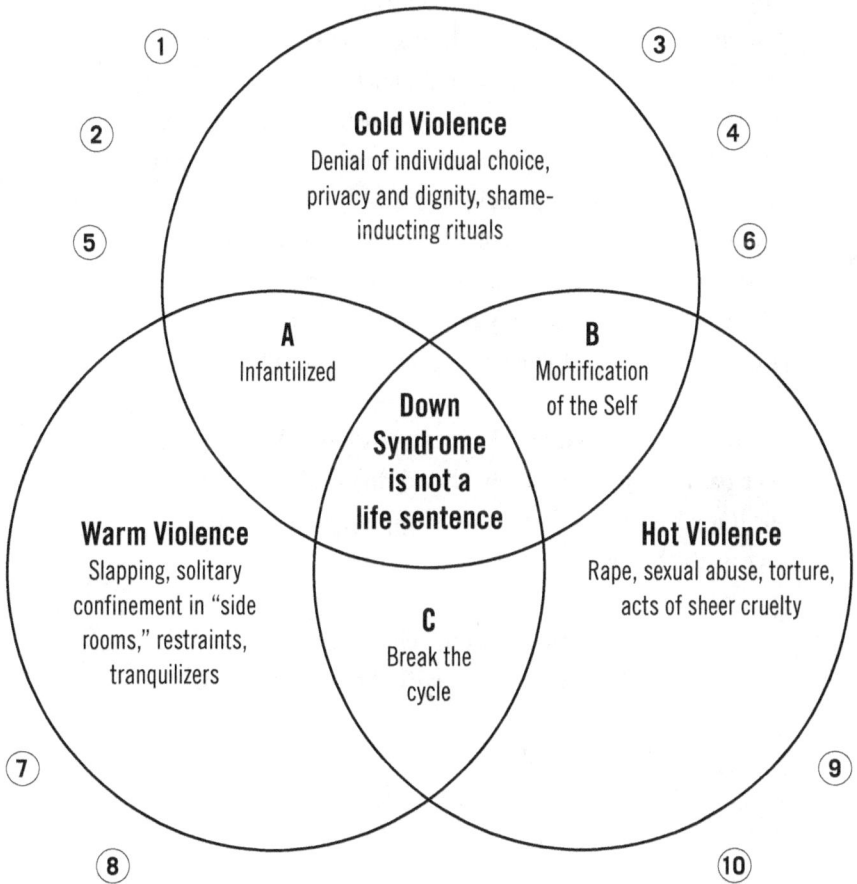

① ② ③ ④ ⑤ ⑥

Cold Violence
Denial of individual choice,
privacy and dignity, shame-
inducting rituals

A
Infantilized

B
Mortification
of the Self

**Down
Syndrome
is not a
life sentence**

Warm Violence
Slapping, solitary
confinement in "side
rooms," restraints,
tranquilizers

C
Break the
cycle

Hot Violence
Rape, sexual abuse, torture,
acts of sheer cruelty

⑦ ⑧ ⑨ ⑩

3) We attended a potluck picnic at our local park, the day bright and blustery. I fought against the wind to hold onto the flimsy paper plates that contained my children's pizza lunch. Another mom joined my picnic blanket to keep me company, and Elyse, who sat in the middle of the blanket, was whining at me, obviously hungry and wanting the pizza in my hand. I needed her to move out of the way so I had room to set the plates down, but before I could ask her to do so, the mom inexplicably attempted to move her for me by grabbing on to her wrist and pulling her up awkwardly by the arm. I was worried she would dislocate Elyse's shoulder. Elyse didn't move anywhere and instead cried out, clutching at her wrist. I can't remember if I said "Stop!" with more than my body, but right away, from the look on my daughter's face, I knew the woman had hurt her.

4) When Elyse cried out that her wrist hurt, the woman dismissed her pain as phantom. "Oh, that didn't really hurt. She's okay." I held my five-year-old, her tears dripping onto my lap, pizza strewn across the blanket.

> B) Mortification of the Self
> Abuse toward persons with disabilities
> reverberates.
> Stripped naked
> A lack of dignity and respect,
> human decency

5) At the beginning of second grade, before the teacher knew her, one of the expectations on Elyse's individualized education plan was to learn the letters of the alphabet. I had it removed.

> Teach her the alphabet again and again
> and again and again and again and again

and again and again and again and again
and again and again and again and again
and again and again and again and again
and again and again and again and again
and again and again and again and again
and again and again and again and again
and again and again and again and again
and again and again and again and again
and again and again and again and again
and again and again and again and again
and again and again and again and again
until she no longer wants to learn anything.

❧

Down syndrome
is not
a life sentence.

6) Her pain is real.
   My pain as her mother is real.

Warm Violence[4]

Warm Violence refers to the way institutions
handle transgressions: slapping, spanking,
solitary confinement in "side rooms,"
restraints, and tranquilizers.

7) The worst thing I've ever physically done to Elyse is slap her little
cheek. Not hard; not like you'd slap a man who cheated on you, but
hard enough that it stunned us both. She burst into tears.

Before the slap, she had been screaming, screaming, screaming. My husband was away for work, and I had to get the kids to school on time. I needed Elyse to get ready. I had to breastfeed the baby, stay up all night, make the meals, clean the house, pack the lunches, breastfeed the baby again, stay up all night. I needed Elyse to get ready. I needed her to stop screaming. Stop screaming in my face. *Stop.* How could I make her stop? I was slipping past the edge.

8) I apologized afterward. Of course I apologized. I bent down to her level and looked her in the eyes. And she slapped me back.

Hot Violence[5]

> Hot Violence can involve rape, sexual abuse, torture,
> and acts of sheer cruelty with the sole purpose
> of gratifying the person inflicting the pain.

9) Before she could walk, and before we found a caring preschool, two-year-old Elyse was enrolled in a co-op where the teachers were supposed to carry her through the dusty corridors to get from place to place. Inexplicably, I wasn't allowed to visit the classroom, but other parents were. Another parent, disturbed by what she had observed, told me they left my daughter to crawl, face in the dirt. The staff goaded Elyse on from across the hall or stood waiting at the top of the staircase when they thought no one was looking.

10) Correct "bad" behaviour, encourage compliance with the rules.

> C) The past interrupts her future.
> Break the cycle.

✳

Class-action Lawsuits: Huronia, Rideau Regional, and Southwestern Regional Centre. Among the list of twenty-two damages to those institutionalized: pain and suffering; a loss of self-esteem; and feelings of humiliation and degradation. The loss of general enjoyment of life.[6]

Eventually, the woman at the park who grabbed my daughter's wrist apologized to me, *to me*, but never to my daughter.

The year her teacher and therapist wanted to teach her the alphabet, Elyse learned to read simple sentences in a second language.

Department of Health—Mental Health Division

A RECLAMATION

Mentally Defective Patient's History

RECLAMATION: THE PROCESS of claiming something back or
of reasserting a right.

In 2012, somewhere in the bowels of the hospital in a non-
descript whitewashed waiting room, I am twenty-two weeks pregnant. Doctors suspect the baby has Down syndrome. I'm holding a
book, *The Lost Girls*,[1] rereading the same page over and over again,
when I'm interrupted from my reverie by staff asking me to complete a patient history form. Filling out forms will become emblematic of "a problem."

For more than a century, parents who gave birth to babies
with Down syndrome were regularly advised to send their child
into large, multi-purpose residential hospitals — institutions —
under the guise that this was best for the individual and the

family, with the added bonus of keeping "these people" out of the general population. Reports released as early as the 1960s revealed that institutions were rife with neglect, abuse, torture, and violence, and yet several remained open into the 2000s.[2] These compounds were built on the outskirts of town, discouraging parents from visiting their child with a disability, which was certain only to bring up the pain of their child's existence and the stark reality of their living conditions. Far from society's sight, and out of mind.

Several years after my daughter with Down syndrome was born, I read *Shut Away: When Down Syndrome Was a Life Sentence*, by Dr. Catherine McKercher, and learned about Ontario's sad history of institutional violence. Dr. McKercher incorporates a seamless weaving of journalistic research with the tragic narrative of her younger brother, Bill, who had Down syndrome and was sent away from their family as a toddler and placed under the guardianship of the Smiths Falls Hospital School. Dr. McKercher's words filled me with rage, the hot breath of injustice breathing heavy down my neck, bile rising in my throat. The history of institutionalization hit me like a visceral blow because my family was still experiencing its residual devastating effects.

✻

When dropping a child off at Smiths Falls, a parent would fill out several forms. "Mentally Defective Patient History" is one of the forms Dr. McKercher's mother completed in 1958.

✻

Can I reclaim the lost lives of children who were institutionalized and the loss of parenting those children by writing about my daughter's life using this dated form as a template? Will reclaiming the past help me to reclaim my own life in the present?

✳

2012: I'm halfway through my second pregnancy. "Down syndrome, soft marker, repeat ultrasound, blood test": these are the words that stand out in my mind from the phone conversation with the midwife after my twenty-week ultrasound. Fifteen-month-old Ariel builds a wooden block tower with her dad. I repeat the midwife's words, "Down syndrome?"

Dan's eyes find mine; the block tower crashes, to Ariel's delight.

1. Name of patient in full: We shall call her E▨
2. (a) Age: 9 (b) Date and year of birth: 2012 (c) Sex: Female
3. Residence, street and number: I will not give you the answers

      Lot and concession: ▨▨▨▨▨
      Municipality: ▨▨▨▨

✳

It wasn't only children with Down syndrome who were institutionalized. Institutions were used for children and adults who were diagnosed with an intellectual disability, ranging from mild to severe, and sometimes accompanied by a physical disability.

✳

Some of the children were hard-to-place wards of the state from children's aid societies, or young adults who had aged out of care.

The first residents at Smiths Falls were adults who had been in psychiatric facilities.[3]

4. County or district:
5. Length of residence in this municipality:
6. Place of birth:
7. Religious denomination:
8. Racial origin:
9. Marital status (single, married, widowed, divorced, separated):

In 1958, what difficulty prevented the creation of separate forms for parents dropping off their babies and the caregivers arriving with adults to whom "marital status" applied? Did parents of young children need that further slap in the face, that they were dropping their child off with full-grown adults? The reminder that their child might never learn to love another in this ageless, sexless place?

⚹

When we lump individuals with disabilities together in one ageless clump, are we not really saying they will never grow up, anyway? And even when they do, they will remain child-like beings to be infantilized?

⚹

In 2022, I am handed a proposed curriculum by school officials, which focuses on life skills as Elyse heads into grade five. I am to read the program over the summer and assess its appropriateness for my daughter, but I find it hard — forgive me — to get past the first page. The front cover reads: "for ages four to twenty-one." *Four to twenty-one.*

10. Number and ages of children, if any, living or dead:

Slap.

11. If not born in Canada, give:

(a) Date of entry into Canada: ▮▮▮▮▮
(b) Port of entry: ▮▮
(c) Name of vessel or railroad on which patient entered: ▮▮

12. Family history:

2012: Waiting in the genetics clinic where we will be taken to another, smaller sterile room to officially receive our daughter's diagnosis, where I am trying and failing to read a book, I am asked to fill out a family history form. I've come from the ultrasound clinic on the floor above, where I was given a similar form.

Every form is biased in that it reflects the needs and goals of its makers.

Could the various medical clinics simply share the information? I can barely concentrate; my hand holding the pen is shaking. These questions, some of them with their probing nature, dig into me like knives. I wonder, are the lengthy forms a way to distract parents from reality? What is our reality? And what are their needs and goals?

Down syndrome is a naturally occurring genetic arrangement. A tiny percentage, less than 1 percent of individuals, inherit this arrangement from their parents. Down syndrome just happens.[4]

(a) Paternal grandparents — name, age, occupation. If dead, age and cause: ▆▆, ▆, ▆▆▆▆▆▆▆▆▆▆▆▆▆

(b) Maternal grandparents — name, age, occupation. If dead, age and cause: ▆▆, ▆, ▆▆▆▆▆▆▆▆▆▆▆▆▆

(c) Father — name, age, birthplace, school grade reached and age, occupation. If dead, age and cause: Dr. D. Purdham; B.Sc., Ph.D. in Pharmacology; Medical Director

(d) Mother — maiden name, age, birthplace, school grade reached and age, occupation before marriage. If dead, age and cause: A. Purdham; B.A., B.Ed., MFA; Writer, Professor.

Can our collective degrees, mine and my husband's, shield our daughter from perceptions of an inferior intelligence? If I go back to school now and complete a Doctor of Philosophy, will our daughter fare better in life, with two doctorate parents? Will more degrees protect her from negative perceptions about people with Down syndrome?

If so, I will do it.

※

Before Elyse was born, I was a classroom teacher. I taught six-year-olds to read and write in a second language. Now, I teach creative writing to university students and work with adults who write their stories, and I write my own.

※

Under "Mother" (only) is the interesting choice of phrasing, "Occupation *before* marriage," the assumption being that after marriage comes homemaker, and employment of any other kind for a woman is untenable. This notion of woman bound to home persists, especially for the mother to a child with a disability. The assumption is that said child will be more work in a society that offers inadequate supports. More work for the mother.

※

Baby Elyse is upstairs, sleeping after a busy visit with family. I'm standing at the foot of the staircase, talking to a close family member. Our relationship is imbued with love, and I'm seeking their approval. I don't think I'll be going back to classroom teaching, I say.

"I think I'm going to write," I proclaim, projecting my future. The family member looks at me, incredulous. "About *what*?"

※

(e) Brothers and sisters: Two sisters. One older, one younger. In order of birth, living or dead:

Give the name, age:
If dead, age and cause:
School grade reached and the age on leaving school:

13. Give age of parents at marriage:

We married in our twenties. A common misconception is that only older mothers give birth to babies with Down syndrome, but the twenty-somethings have the most babies. Those younger than thirty-five give birth to the most babies with Down syndrome.[5] I gave birth to Elyse at twenty-eight years old. I was a new mom at twenty-seven; our family was complete when I was thirty-one.

14. Are father and mother blood relations?

I'm standing in my backyard talking to a neighbour whose dog, a 140-pound Great Dane, comes to call on my dog. The play is rough. Once, the neighbour's dog jumps up to greet me, hitting my face, and the force of the dog's weight slits my cheek like a punch, blood pouring out. During our visits, I make small talk with the owner, who's middle-aged, ex-military. We're exchanging travel stories and I tell them about attending the World Down Syndrome Congress in India in 2014, two years after Elyse was born.

"Do you know why the Congress was held in India? Why it was special that it was there?" The questions are rhetorical, my tone friendly. I don't mean for them to answer.

"Must be because of all the in-breeding and incest," they suppose.

I stand there, dumbfounded.

"No," I quickly recover, "it's because with such a large population, India has the most people with Down syndrome in the world, some thirty-two million."

I say this matter-of-factly, like they haven't just insulted me with racist ignorance and condescension.

To clarify, there is no connection between Down syndrome and incest and there never has been.

✳

15. Have any relatives been mentally ill, feeble-minded, epileptic, neurotic, eccentric? Give particulars: ▓▓▓▓▓▓
▓▓▓▓▓▓▓▓▓▓▓▓▓

16. Personal and development history:

(a) Was birth of patient full term? ▓▓▓▓▓▓▓▓▓

(b) Was birth natural, prolonged or difficult?
████████████████████

(c) Were instruments used? ████████████████████████

(d) Was there injury at birth? ███████████████████████

(e) Were there any convulsions associated with, or shortly after birth? ██

(f) Was patient breast or bottle fed?

After not feeding orally for the first two weeks of her life, Elyse breastfed until she was three years old. The day after her birth, she needed surgery to remove an atresia in her digestive tract; specifically, a blockage of the duodenum, part of the small intestine. After surgery, she was tube fed — "plant fertilizer," as the NICU nurse called it — for two weeks, through a nasogastric tube in her nose that ran directly to her stomach. On the fourth day of Elyse's life, my milk came in and my breasts wept. I longed to nurse her. Instead, I pumped eight times a day. Once her incision healed enough and I could try breastfeeding, Elyse took to my engorged breasts slowly, then voraciously, the way she would later devour books. The sensation of babe to breast was orgasmic, like the relief of scratching a worsening itch. Like collecting hair off the nape of a neck on a humid day. Gloves to frozen hands. Exactly like blinking the tears back, then allowing them to fall, sweet release. Mercy.

With one swipe, Elyse eventually ripped the feeding tube out herself.

"I'm taking her home," I told our medical team who called her recovery "remarkable," after four and a half weeks in hospital. I called it love.

Some fifty years ago, babies with Elyse's intestinal condition were left to die. They effectively starved to death.

   (g) Describe any feeding defects in the first two years:
       �ढ▓▓▓▓▓▓▓▓

   (h) Age at which first tooth appeared: ▓

   (i) Give age patient began to walk:

I have a candid video of Elyse learning to walk. In the video, she stands to shake out a small, fuchsia, princess-patterned handmade quilt, copying the motions of her big sister, who's holding a baby blanket and standing in front of her. Elyse flies the mini princess quilt in front of herself like a cape, then crouches to lay it flat on the ground. Once the quilt is in place, Elyse stands, then leans forward and takes her first step onto the uneven squares I hand-stitched, her arms poised like a tightrope walker. Her step is epic, monumental, of superhuman proportion. One giant leap for humankind. Her sister and I clap and cheer as Elyse tumbles onto her backside, again and again, with each attempt. Elyse joins her hands together in glee, imitating our movements, then repeats the motions: stand from squat, fan the blanket like a matador, lay it flat, step onto it, fall onto her backside.

   (j) Give age patient began to talk: ▓

   (k) Is there any speech defect now present?
       ▓▓▓▓▓▓▓▓▓▓

   (l) Is present gait normal, awkward or shuffling? ▓

17. School history:

   (a) Age began school:

Elyse attends a French first-language school, though we are English speakers at home. Her understanding of the French language is good. When I visited the small school of fewer than 150 students, there was already another student with Down syndrome. "She'll get one hundred percent support," the principal assured me. And she does. An educational assistant supports Elyse's learning one on one, as needed, for the entirety of the school day.

(b) Grade or class reached. Give age on leaving school: ■

(c) Reasons for leaving school:

When choosing a school for Elyse as she was heading into kindergarten, I visited a public school with a French immersion program before visiting the French first-language school. I was a French immersion teacher. I attended French immersion myself as a child, and so did my husband. Elyse's grandma and aunt taught French. Suffice it to say, we wanted our children to go to a French-language school. At the only French immersion school in town, I asked to meet with the resource teacher.

"What supports are available for a child with Down syndrome in the French immersion program?" I asked.

"Hmm," she said, hand to chin, "that's a great question."

(d) If never attended school, give reasons: ■

(e) Has patient had auxiliary class training? ■

(f) Can patient read and write? ■■■

18. Economic history: Has patient ever earned wages? If so, state type of work, how long employed, wages earned and reasons for leaving.

See above re. *slap.*

19. Social history:

(a) What are the patient's interests or amusements? ▓▓▓▓
(b) Has patient playmates? If so, are they of the same age or sex
     or are they younger?

When we moved towns, Elyse began at a new school. For her
ninth birthday that year, we invited her entire grade three and four
class to the park behind our house for her party. Though they'd
known her for only a few months, every single kid in the class arrived. The kids ran and screamed and played joyously together, with
Elyse at the centre of the fray. As her parents, we were heart-filled to
bursting, overjoyed and grateful.

But then the invitation wasn't reciprocated.

Who is responsible for inclusion? As children, we understand
the importance of belonging. Why is it that a kindness — devoting
time to attending a party — goes only so far?

Elyse didn't receive a single invite the rest of the year. Sometimes,
we are slow to change.

The next year, she did.

20. Moral history:

(a) Is there a history of petty thieving or stealing? ▓
(b) Does patient do injury to himself? ▓
(c) Is patient cruel to people or animals? ▓
(d) Is patient a fire-setter? ▓
(e) Describe patient's sex interests and experiences, if any:

What about morality? Babies with Down syndrome were not
forcibly taken from their families by the government, as was the
case with Indigenous children in Canada — and those wrongs can

never be righted. But isn't social pressure a kind of force? I support a woman's right to her own body. A right to choose what is right for her and her family. I'm advocating for balanced information to accompany prenatal testing and a society that doesn't automatically assume a mother would choose to abort or abandon a disabled child. I'm advocating for increased financial support for those who need it and for essential services to be more readily available.

Isn't social pressure the kind of force families still experience today? The kind that gets fetuses with Down syndrome killed?

*

2012: We wait in the small, sterile room for the obstetrician to arrive and deliver the fate of our child. The doctor is kind in giving the news that our baby has Down syndrome. She waits a beat, then adds:

"Now, I have to ask this ... do you want an abortion?"

21. Habits:

(a) Can patient dress and undress self? ▓
(b) Can patient feed self? Is feeding cleanly? ▓
(c) Does patient wet or soil bed or clothing? ▓
(d) Does patient sleep well at night? ▓
(e) Has patient any preference in foods? ▓
(f) Can patient go up and down stairs unaided? ▓
(g) Describe character traits. Is patient quarrelsome, quick or violent tempered, suggestible, stubborn, seclusive, suspicious, obedient, etc.?

Elyse's favourite food is the starry-eyed blueberry. And pizza. She loves cheese pizza. Her bedtime routine involves teeth, toilet, tub, jammies, stories, and leaving the hall light on so she doesn't feel scared of the dark. Elyse doesn't like to be left alone. After stories and lights out, Dan sits in the hallway, playing on his phone, biding time. In the company of her dad, mom, two sisters, kitten, puppy, and what I can only call feeling loved, Elyse slowly drifts off to sleep.

No further questions.

_____

(signature of medical practitioner)

_____

(address)

Date: _____

NATURE

Untethered

SITTING ON MY cottage dock, I'm trying to figure out what it means to be alone. I've left my family behind: three girls, one husband, and one rambunctious dog — my Vizsla, Louie — to embark on a ten-day writing residency as part of my MFA. I used to crave being alone and, at the beginning of the pandemic, wanted nothing more than to get away. I sat inside at my swirling desk chair in my bedroom, in Zoom room after Zoom room, resisting that one coveted button on the screen — LEAVE — with my family pressing in around me on all sides. LEAVE, that red button seemed to pulse at me from the corner of my eye, no matter how engaging the session, no matter how hard I concentrated on the camera. LEAVE. GO. I wanted nothing more. But where? For a time, nowhere felt safe, and then over the course of a year, I grew accustomed to the noise, the busy-ness of bodies in the background, the constant hovering over my shoulder. I stayed and learned to write through it, into it. Still, when it came time to LEAVE, I knew I would be ready. I was pining for freedom.

On my long drive up to the cottage, I encountered a plethora of wild animals. I stopped halfway to visit my parents and spotted a hummingbird outside my mother's kitchen window. I watched its wings flutter, willing my heart to still. As a little girl, I would watch the hummingbird feeder outside my grandmother's kitchen window, my mom's mom, and it was she who first pointed to the creature, which reminds me of a flying seahorse. My grandmother's been gone nearly ten years now, but as I took in the humming-bird, she felt close. Temporality is an illusion; time skips over itself, overlaps, repeats like beating wings perpetually in motion. The hummingbird stayed a while, hovered here and there, and then, momentarily, alit on a branch. Paused, before taking flight again.

Back on the road to the cottage, I spotted a turtle. Then another one, and another one! The thrill of seeing wildlife never gets old. When I arrived at the cottage, tires crunched against the gravel. I unpacked my bags and noticed a merganser floating in the water beside the dock. The auburn feathers on its head, reminiscent of a mohawk, made the sea duck unmistakable.

I appreciate something about spotting an animal in the wild; I like to think it's my keen eye, but maybe there's more to it. A wild creature can roam wherever it likes. Should it not wish to be seen, it can remain hidden. Perhaps that is why, when I see something like a hummingbird or a turtle, I am the one who feels seen. Like I have been chosen, rather than the one doing the choosing from a shelter or a breeder. Nature chooses me. Our wilds coincide.

That night at the cottage, I'm invited to sit around a neighbour's fire, and a polyphemus moth flaps its way into the party, dancing in the lights my neighbours have strung in the trees, flailing about as though it's looking for something or someone. Its size alone — bigger than my hand — is impressive. The moon above us, my neighbour holds up his phone for me to see what I'm looking at, what is looking at me. "This is what they look like up close," he says. Two huge owl eyes blink back at me, etched in tissue-paper wings. Nature, meta-nature, staring back, protecting itself from becoming prey.

The next day, sitting on the cottage dock, I struggle to let the words push through. I have had a day of Zoom meetings and online sessions, and too many images flash in my face and a cacophony of voices compete in my head, all talking at once. I spot a dock spider, or does the dock spider see me? Smell me? Feel my vibrations? When I turn my head in his direction, he leaps below, a jump that looks more like a glide, and tucks himself in between the crevasse of old boards out of view. Nature frees my attention from the haze of the screen. Shortly, I'm feeling hot and decide to go for a swim. Beneath the wavy water, the fish that hang around our dock are out of view, but I know they're there.

I stuff the waxy balls of silicon in my ears and jump off the lilting dock with the grace of a well-fed duck. Actual decoy ducks float ceaselessly to my far right, marking the waterline alongside my neighbour's dock. I veer left, away from the ducks, using a breast-stroke, propelling, reaching, kicking my way toward the floating dock off in the distance.

The swim out to the floating dock, due west, isn't that far; I'm looking at it now, squinting from my place on my dock as the sun dazzles on top of the water late in the day. It's a hundred feet, maybe. I'm not sure. I don't know distances the way I understand time, except that one holds steady while the other seems to fold and dip, collapse, expand.

It's a two-and-a-half-minute swim to the floating dock. As I reach the finish line, a loon previously obscured by the dock pops into view, just on the other side. Surprised to find it so close to me — forty feet, maybe; less than a minute's swim at a leisurely pace — I stop swimming and allow myself to just bob there in the water, admiring the bird. The loon has chosen me. This isn't the first time the loon and I have paused to look each other in the eye. I admire its fidelity to this lake.

I stare down into the undulating waves, black velvet, pen in parallel movement against the page, rising and falling. Across the shore from me — five or six hundred metres; a kilometre? — stands the point of white pines. White clouds drift by overhead. The trouble with judging distance in water is that things appear closer than they actually are.

Bobbing there in the water, the loon close to me, I can make out its fine features, the ebony feathers and lace collar. Without a sound, the loon dips its head and disappears into the water for … how long? Five seconds? I'm in the open expanse of water, some indeterminate distance from shore. Not that far. But farther than it looks. I think, what if the loon were to resurface in the exact spot where I'm swimming? I momentarily tuck myself into a tight ball. The loon wouldn't do that, though, would he? His wild wants nothing to do with my wild.

Every time I encounter a loon, I hear my friend Megan's reverent voice from decades ago when we were teenagers, visiting her cottage. "It's very rare," she said, "for loons to get close. They're shy birds." And she taught me how to call them, a whistling sound between two pressed thumbs, cupped hands, an approximation of their guttural cry. But I don't call my wild birds at all. They come to me.

The loons resurface to my right, to the northwest. I say "loons" because now there are two, as though diving down and resurfacing with one's mate is exactly how it's done. "Like this," he's saying, with every proud feather on his body. If he was forty feet away before, now he's ten feet away, with his mate. Ten feet. But here's the thing: the loon didn't *actually* pick me. The loons drew nearer. They leaned in. And we studied one another up close. We were tame to each other, our wilds coinciding.

The moment has passed. The loons see I'm doing nothing but bobbing and gawking at them, calculating my luck and our distance for what it's worth, and so they move on, dive down away from me, but still tethered to this lake.

I will think of the loons as my pets, I console myself on the swim back. The best pets I ever had. I don't have to feed them or make them come to me or train them.

Emerging from the water back on the dock, I stand upright, then fold myself in half, hair dangling from my head between my legs. I lie down on the dock and tilt my head all the way back and find it hard to identify which way is the sky. Pine trees stand tall in the water. Reflections become more real than reality.

In thinking of the loons, I'm filled with a twinge of regret, a wave of sadness and pity for the contained existence lived by my dog, who seems more inclined toward freedom than a domestic life. Louie is a Vizsla, a breed of dog notorious for its exuberance and playfulness, abundant energy and willingness to hunt. Louie is wild, which is precisely what I like about him, though he's hard to train and control, which is supposedly the primary job of a pet owner. I'd prefer to just love him, keep him wild the way he was made. I believe in obedience as love, but it's not exactly how I'm built. I'm better suited to keeping wild things that aren't for keeping at all, but that keep me.

I think, like with time instead of distance, I'm better with wild things. This knowledge has done nothing to curb my enthusiasm as a pet owner. I'm better with wild things that get me in the water, invite me into their habitat, their world; that dive down to dark places I can't reach. But it is in taming our pets that we ourselves are tamed.

Sitting on my cottage dock, I'm figuring out what it means to be connected — to Louie, to those loons, and to my family. Author Eula Biss writes, "We are continuous with everything here on Earth. Including, and especially, each other."[1] In a way, the birds devour me. I am the birds, the birds are me; they eat the insects that sup on my flesh. In a way, I'm nature's pet; the sky is holding me up, rather than down, and the river is the source from which I flow. In a way, I am wild too.

Nature keeps me wild by making me feel seen; I'm like those loons, free to go where I please, pet to no one.

Having a pet and being among nature reminds me that my time here is finite, though some part of me will live on. Time may bend, shift and sway, but once I'm gone, head below water, who knows where I'll resurface, or how far?

Louie helps keep me tethered to my home, to my human family and familiar waters. My pet reminds me that freedom and space to oneself is a gift, but that so is connection, family, togetherness — being tamed. So is the option to RETURN.

On day four, especially, of my ten-day residency, I miss my tame life back home and I know it is precisely because I am free to leave. Perched on the edge of the cottage dock, the memory of my family members lands like a flock of birds settling on the branches of my heart. They alight there, rest a while, and I hold them close, comforted, remembering I know the way home.

Wild Horses

Life is a window of vulnerability.[1]

— Donna Haraway

THE DAY IS clear and bright; white clouds dot the sky — perfect driving weather to visit a friend on her farm. I pass by large fields with enormous swaths of black fabric covering the soil. I drive by an older woman tinkering in her garden, whose head shoots up reflexively as I pass. I look straight ahead, two hands on the steering wheel, at the pair of birds in front of me. *Killdeers, maybe? Move.* The birds strike me as lovers lingering in the other's company, reluctant to be torn apart. I notice the pin-straight legs, the speedy steps, and the curvature of the wing. As I approach their resting place, with my body and my mind I will them to fly — and they do as they should, they cast out their sickle-shaped wings, but one of the pair is not fast enough.

I brake the split second before the moment of impact. One of the lovers, hesitant to depart, veers to the right too late. *Thud.* It's as if the bird couldn't quite believe I would actually hit it. I have disrupted the natural order of things. I see its crooked wing in my rear-view mirror. The abrupt violence is a shock to my system. I'm on my way to visit my friend Martha and her new baby; this doesn't bode well. I feel a tingling sense of loss and shame. The older woman tinkering in her front garden, has she seen? I'm not supposed to be here. We're in a pandemic; nobody is supposed to be anywhere. In my state of disarray, I miss my next turn, and have to three-point manoeuvre back in the right direction, toward the deceased — or soon-to-be deceased — bird. Momentarily, I have to face what I've done.

When I arrive, I can't bring myself to tell Martha about the killdeer, to carry the contradictory mood from my car to her full, smiling face, her porcelain-apple cheeks. Martha, a new mother dressed in black, is as luminescent as the moon set against an ebony sky. The intensity of the sun above washes out everything around us. I am immediately swept up by familiar country smells: the dried hay; the heady, floral scent of the front garden and trees in bloom and a hint of manure wafting over from a neighbouring farm. The baby in Martha's arms is plump and fresh, a good eater with a full, bright swath of auburn hair on his head, two months new to this world. She straps him in a carrier close to her chest, covers him in a fine mesh, and shoos away the blackflies that would gladly pierce his tender skin for that warm crimson river that flows beneath.

Martha grew up in the metropolis of Toronto, while I called small-town Peterborough home; both city girls, but on different scales. Martha's husband, Remi, has been a farmer his entire life. He was raised by a father who grew tobacco, but when the tobacco industry fell out of favour and crashed in the late 1990s, Remi began his own ginseng farm.

We begin with a tour of the grounds. Martha guides me through a discreet passageway in the brush, leading me to the hen house.

Martha and I are fellow students pursuing our MFA, and this is the first time I've come out to her farm to meet her in person. We visit with the boys, Dmytro (pronounced "Dmytri"), a white rooster; Boris, a red rooster — Martha's favourite; and Tango, a guinea hen who keeps crossing the road and "needs to be kept in line," according to Martha's mother-in-law, before she goes the way of the two barn kittens, splat against the road.

Human invention is unkind to animals.

Then there is Mango, the other guinea hen, who spends a couple of weeks a year hiding in the bushes, protecting a nest and willing eggs to come that never will — not without male guineas around. In her recent state of protecting and delivering her own egg, Martha tells me she finds Mango's behaviour upsetting, and as a mother who loves her chicks, so do I. Guinea fowl are hard to come by in the pandemic, Martha explains. "Everyone is trying to be a farmer."

After a quick stop at the rabbit hutch, where a large thumper lounges, we leave the grass pellets and urine odour behind us and make our way over to an adjacent field, through scrubby grass and more brush, the sun a hot blaze of fire in the sky, heat thick in the air radiating down on our faces and shoulders. We arrive at a faded white outbuilding the length of a rowboat. My friend opens the door and says, "Look," as though letting me in on a secret. I smell their avian musk before I spot them. Inside, in the front right corner, under a heat lamp, are ten baby chicks. They scurry away from me, peeping, and huddle together as a pack, their yellow fluff as delicate as snowflakes.

"Can I hold one?"

A large bumblebee buzzes against the windowpane, bumping into itself over and over again. Martha, who seems disturbed by the noise, steps back outside the shed with her baby, the door left open. She will later tell me the pungent whiff of excrement and sweaty animal bodies assaulting our noses forced her out.

"Sure." She does not follow up with instructions of care or caution. Remi, her husband, has brought her these chicks — they belong to Martha and Remi— and she is happy to share them with me.

"You hold one and I'll take your picture," she says.

❋

I took care of chicks once as a practice teacher. My mentor, a kindergarten teacher, had chicks that needed caring for over the weekend. I ended up with three. By nightfall of their arrival, two had died. Dan and I believed they died of fright and blamed our two dogs. We rushed the last chick back to my mentor with the larger brood to keep it company. A chick will die on its own, perhaps of loneliness.

While visiting a pet shop as a child of seven or eight, I was granted permission to handle a hamster pup. Almost immediately, the pup wiggled from my grasp and went careening to the floor, a suicidal leap. I was horrified and quickly scooped it up from where it had landed on the tile and passed it back to the teenage employee without saying anything. The hamster may have died, or at least been rendered paralyzed by my inexperience. I won't make the same mistake twice.

❋

I'm awkward about the chicks. "Do I just grab one? Can I step in here?" I place one foot inside their box, which sends up a cacophony of alarm, their peeps ringing out. Knowing they won't hurt me, I narrow in on one and go for it. With animals, I decide, it's best to be quick and decisive. Any hesitation on my part would be to admit defeat, lose trust and respect. The chick I capture has no recourse but to peep as loudly as it possibly can, while the others fall

148

completely silent, as though willing themselves to disappear while also listening intently to the alarm of their sibling.

Martha snaps my photo, while I hold the little darling securely in my palms, up close to my face and out in front where I can see it. Fresh life in my hands. I gently ease the little chick back into its brood, who rally around. I joke about wanting to take one home for my daughter's birthday. Martha seems indifferent to my statement, as though she'd almost say yes had I insisted bravely enough, and perhaps by way of excuse for this behaviour offers, "Only five or six will likely survive." I'm surprised — *on a farm?* I thought the death of the kindergarten chicks was something I'd done.

Next, I meet her mother-in-law, who has just arrived in her truck and is now tending to the garden, the strawberry patch planted the night before. *Was she the woman by the road? Has she been anticipating my arrival, only to be disappointed by my callousness?* Her mother-in-law pauses from her work only long enough to greet me, then her eyes shift back to the soil, the labour at hand. We inhabit different worlds.

Martha and I take refuge in the front yard in the company of the chickens, under the shade of an endangered eastern flowering dogwood, a gnarled tree with white blossoms. Its fragrance is intoxicating.

When Boris, Martha's favourite red rooster, lets out a series of cock-a-doodle-dos, the sound strikes me as familiar. I feel at home among his calls. My ancestors were Ontario farmers. My maternal grandfather grew up on a cattle farm referred to as "The Ranch." My mom collected chicken eggs from her aunt's farm as a child, those dainty yet durable orbs smooth and warm in her hands. Squeeze one end to end and the shell will never break. Tip the egg on its side, crack, and out come its gooey contents. My grandmother fed nine mouths and kept a huge garden that she planted at the end of a depression and tended into her eighties, a time when her granddaughter's baby — my daughter Ariel — could sit on her lap. As a child, I pulled carrots dripping with soil from the earth, dined on beets the colour of deep bruises from my grandmother's garden. The bittersweet tang of crunchy rhubarb tickled my tongue.

Dirt flows through my veins. The visit to Martha's farm has unearthed something within me; I experience a kind of ancestral déjà-vu. I've never been here before but the deeply buried memories I hold inside tell me otherwise; my awakened sense of awe reveals a different story, one of an enduring connection to the natural world. My ancestors were stewards of the land, and while they turned the soil for good or for bad, I have lost that responsibility. I am cut off from my roots. But I haven't totally forgotten, and here, in this place, those deep memories are taking seed.

Martha leaves her baby behind with Grandma and we call her goldendoodle, Snowball, to go for a walk in the forest. He mouths my arm playfully, demanding my attention. Martha takes me through the back fields, which smell of freshly thawed earth, and out to a forest where we finally duck into the shade.

"Look," she tells me, another secret. Pink trilliums, ablaze, litter the forest floor, their petals dimming like distant stars. "I didn't want our visit to wait even one more week, or we'd miss them."

The maple trees high above offer green shelter below. Martha's farm uncoils before me like a scroll; she unfurls nature's gifts one at a time.

For ten years, Martha was an airline stewardess who worked on private jets and was used to rolling with the rich and famous. She had once been the personal flight attendant of Bruce Springsteen. She's a woman with star power and charisma. She traded in her glamorous life for a simpler, traditional pathway.

"I had this moment last year," Martha says, "sitting on the front stoop, pregnant, watching the chickens, thinking *this is my life now*. I might have been barefoot too. Barefoot and pregnant." She lets out a deep sigh with a telling smile. She's become the stereotypical farmer's wife and she is radiant. This new life suits her.

Driving home, I will think about how living among nature, with nature, caring for animals and being with animals, potentially suits everyone. It's in our nature — we *are* nature. I want to belong on this farm, with these animals, but it's not the context in which I grew up. As a species, humans are constantly trying to change, to tame, to work against the patterns that exist around us, patterns that have always existed; that will continue to exist long after we are gone. City life has eroded my understanding of myself. Something about the fresh country air, the woodsy scent, and the wide-open space make me see myself more keenly.

Martha and Remi plan to live off their garden's bounty and exchange goods with other farmers. Martha explains how the local school children used to be given time off school to collect harvest in the fall with their families, but now it's uniform government-mandated hours in the classroom across the province, no matter the realities of how we come by our food. Our curriculum holds no space for the natural world around us and how to care for it; now, only what's in our heads seems to matter. We, the self-conscious, egocentric species.

Martha tells me how wild ginseng is found naturally across Ontario. The mixed sandy soil of Norfolk County, where she lives, creates perfect growing conditions. "You can usually find it growing side by side with trilliums in the spring. Look for a plant with red berries. Ginseng is the root."

The word "ginseng" is derived from the Chinese *rénshēn*, where *rén* means "person" and *shēn* means "plant root."[2] I look up photos and see ginseng leaves naturally shaped in the form of a flower, the tan roots like naked dancing bodies swaying beneath the soil with their elegant, elongated limbs. Ginseng is coveted in China for its energizing qualities and properties that protect from viruses and flush out toxins in the body. Pre-pandemic, Remi travelled frequently to Asia for business, but Martha the airline stewardess and Remi didn't meet on a plane, as one might surmise. They met ballroom dancing.

Back under the shade of the endangered dogwood, I inhale the aroma of my ginseng tea as Martha explains the root to me.

"It's an acquired taste," she warns me beforehand. "Earthy."

My first sip is like a jolt. "Tastes kind of like peanuts," I say.

Later, my pharmacologist husband will say to me, "Isn't ginseng like a drug? Sorry, I shouldn't say that — it's *natural*. But it's a stimulant for sure, an upper."

In addition to being a potent antioxidant, ginseng increases brain function, boosts the immune system, and combats tiredness by increasing energy levels.[3] A powerful punch for one little root.

To farm a crop of ginseng takes four or five years, and once a crop is successful, the same soil can never be used for ginseng again because of replant disease, which causes the second crop's roots to rot and crumble. On my drive down, it was the ginseng fields I spotted along the highway, with the large swathes of black fabric that offer essential shade overhead, mimicking the tree cover conditions Martha and I walked under in the forest.

I can't stop smiling. From holding the baby chick, to Boris's crowing, to sitting in the shade on a hot day with my friend and her new baby, sipping tea and simply enjoying the day and conversing. Or maybe it's the effects of the ginseng tea, branching like roots through my body. I have missed company dearly, but I've also missed the world. The sweet-smelling air, grass beneath my feet, chickens over yonder.

"It's beautiful here," I tell her, still smiling. I've tried to imagine my life in the country. But I can't, not really.

In just over one short year, Martha has gotten married, given birth, and settled into this life. She's made local friends in a pandemic. One even named their baby Martha. She's learned to be more observant. I watch her noticing the world around us.

"Life is fragile," she says, "but also robust." And as I look around, the whole scene is alive, pulsing sky, branches and grasses swaying with gentle movements, tremors, chickens and insects, pecks and flight, supple skin. The baby once again nestled into its mother.

We are undeniably one. Undeniably fragile and robust.

On my drive home, I watch carefully for birds. I drive the speed limit, eighty kilometres an hour, and as suddenly as the birds that showed up on my arrival, a car flashes its lights at me and next comes a blue Ford pickup truck with a muscled man, clearly a local farmer, waving his strong arm out of the window, his hand gesturing emphatically, pleading, *slow down.*

In the distance, a car is pulled off to the side of the road. I slow right down and see what the fuss is about.

Two golden horses have escaped from their fenced field.

The sight of the horses grazing free before me at the side of the highway is unnatural, but so obviously right and natural, simultaneously. One of the horses rears back on its hind legs, as though it's having a rollicking good time; the other dips his head into the long grasses to feast. These wild beasts are free, as they should be, but of course they should not be free because they are not wild beasts — they have been tamed. The owner, an older, wide-bellied man, pads down his long drive toward them; his wife, hands out at her side in alarm, stands back by the door to their home. The horses appear to be laughing, having the time of their lives.

I once read a story about a boy who spooked a horse in a stadium and the steed went careening out of the racetrack and onto a busy highway, where it was struck by a car. In colliding with the car, the horse killed the teenage driver behind the wheel. The horse, badly damaged by the crash, also had to be put down.

Our actions have consequences. We barrel ahead on this planet, strange stallions in saucy suits, having the time of our lives, eating the fresh grass beside the highway, taking more than our fair fill; or scared as hell, running away from our past into an unknown future, blazing a trail of wreckage as we go. We are wild horses on a collision course.

I understand, immediately upon seeing the horses, why I have been alerted to their presence by my fellow drivers. A horse, running free, can kill. But the farmer's way of life is different from my own. The people around here understand intimately that a human is much more likely to kill than an animal. In that split second, the moment when our paths cross, I am certain that I saw it in the muscled farmer's face, the grace and forcefulness of his arm and countenance: *fragile and robust*, gentle yet strong. It was not my safety he was worried for. He was looking out for the horses.

A Thin Line

Think, occasionally, of the suffering of which you
spare yourself the sight.[1]

— Albert Schweitzer

WE ARE, ALL of us, made from the stuff of dead stars. The process
is called "stellar nucleosynthesis."[2] When a star dies, it blasts into
stellar bits that travel across galaxies. Half of the particles that make
up our bodies aren't even from the Milky Way,[3] the home of our
solar system, but from a distance beyond its hundred-thousand-
light-year reach.[4] The red in our blood is iron, our crimson filling,
the element that is created the moment before a star explodes.[5] A
star's explosion is known as a supernova; the brightest star in the sky
collapsing under its own weight. Stardust theory holds that every
element on Earth comes from elsewhere, in this way. We are intergalactic glitter that's made its way to Earth. Without the sun, our
closest star and ally, we would die. We are dependent on its light, its
warmth, on its process of making our plants photosynthesize into

food. We are also reliant on the water that evaporates in its light and cycles back. Water that dates back further than the sun, that is older, wiser.[6] Water that holds memory through the patterns of its molecules, that remembers where it's been, what it touches, and when we arrived. With the sun, we are also only one thin sheath away, each of us, from burning.

❋

I see her as I drive past, stumbling down the street, decrepit. *Please*, I think, *I don't want us to run into her.* She is a mess. I'm Ronald from *The Paper Bag Princess*: "… You are a mess! You smell like ashes, your hair is all tangled, and you are wearing a dirty old paper bag. Come back when you are dressed like a real princess."[7] I don't want an encounter with somebody who's visibly dishevelled, broken. I have two bright-eyed ten-year-olds in the back of my SUV, one blond, one brunette: best friends, gigglers. They are naive and sheltered, in need of protection. How would I explain this woman to them?

We are on our way to the cottage. The SUV is packed full. The girls have their cupholders folded down in anticipation of the bottles of iced tea I will be buying them to go with their dinner. We planned for pitas, but a thunderstorm has knocked out power in that block of downtown. We reroute to hit up a treat shop first: Black Honey, the best dessert place in town.

I park the car and notice the Freshii on the corner. "What about Freshii? You girls can get bowls."

While these girls have not yet been exposed to the ways of the world, the underworld, they are well versed in the vernacular of a privileged life. They speak the dialect of healthy takeout well. As do I. Even though there will be no pitas — no power, no pitas — the girls and I can afford to cruise around until we find an open takeout place that suits our tastes. This idea of accessibility to food as an immense privilege will sit with me and my uneaten burrito, afterward, when I find I no longer have an appetite.

We agree to order Freshii, but cross the street to check out Black Honey first.

As we cross Hunter Street, directly in front of us is the woman, doubled over, one arm across her abdomen, the other flailing to the side. She's walking backward for a few steps, and I think I can see her bare bum, a pale moon rising from below her ill-fitting T-shirt. The woman, the one I didn't want to see, faces me, looking me directly in the eyes as I reach the curb on her side of the street. We're standing in front of a store. The sign reads "Convenience: Variety, Smokes and Cigars."

"Please, can you help me?"

She asks for money, and I immediately reach for my wallet and pull out a loonie, the only coin I have. Why have I not pulled out a bill? Is it because I believe she will use it on drugs or alcohol instead of food? *Yes.*

The woman is wet, and the hair on her head — what is left of it — is pulled into a straggly ponytail to one side, held by a wide, faded elastic band. Her pants are black capris, torn at the edges around her shins like rags. The purple design around the top shows these were once someone's activewear. The workout pants hang loose around her emaciated frame. Her navy-blue shirt is dotted with silver bunnies, their decals long since fading, peeling away. She herself seems to be fading, disappearing, rubbed away. Easy prey.

"I need help," she repeats. "I'm scared."

With the enunciation of her fear, that is it. The thin sheath between us slips away and the world stops for her and me. Our lines cross, her path and mine, like asteroids colliding, an intergalactic event. I feel the presence of the girls over my left shoulder, standing stone still, watching. If I turn my back on this woman and hurry the girls away, it will be like turning a shoulder on myself, on my daughter, on my daughter's friend, on the very stardust I am made of.

"Do you need to go to a shelter?" I ask her. Clearly, I think she needs to go to a shelter. She can't stay here, at the corner of Hunter and Aylmer, outside this convenience store that sells cigars.

"Yes," she agrees. "Can you call for me?" She asks as though she's seven years old, needing a shoe tied. Not in a baby voice, but resigned, knowing she can't quite do it herself.

On my iPhone, I quickly google the number for the shelter.

She has a noticeable blond moustache above her upper lip and her exposed legs are ravaged with hair that seems to cling like moss at the edge of a cliff. The V-neck of her top reveals some long-since-forgotten tattoo inscription across the left side of her chest, below her collarbone, tucked above her heart. Art fits somewhere after basic survival in the hierarchy of needs. I wonder what the tattoo says? But it no longer seems important.

"It's so good to see kids," she says, squeezing her eyes shut, then opening them. "It's been so long since I've seen any kids."

I'm half listening to her now as I've got my ear to the phone, calling the shelter. She mumbles something I don't quite catch, about a child — her child? I can't be sure, though in another sense, I am sure. I see her confusion. Where is this baby/child now? Not hers. Gone, as though disappeared through a black hole.

She closes her eyes, opens them, shuts them. Another universe away. I can't attend to her suffering in this moment, so I stay silent. The momentous event that is the loss of her child sits between us. The phone continues to ring unanswered; my girls look on.

Springing into action is what privileged women like me know how to do. We ascertain the problem and create a plan. My plan is to call the shelter. Make sure this woman is safe. Show my kids that I care, that we should all care, that a person in need is a person in need. That we don't turn our backs on a person in need, no matter how destitute, forgotten, and discarded they seem. Especially when that is the case. *Why is that the case?* And why do I need to remind myself of this?

We are new to town. This scene is new to us. Where we came from, homelessness and drug addiction remained hidden and unseen, absent from our streets. Here, drug addicts and prostitutes roam in broad daylight. The city is facing a methamphetamine and opioid crisis.

My friend's father volunteered at the men's shelter in town during Covid-19. With the world shut down, job loss at a premium, drug use exploded. Her dad witnessed four men overdose. One died while he was waiting for paramedics to arrive and he was in the middle of giving chest compressions, mouth-to-mouth resuscitation. Her dad took a two-week mental health leave as a result and on the day he returned, another man overdosed and died right in front of him. He had to take a permanent leave from his volunteer duties after that.

At the same time that drug addiction, mental health issues, homelessness, and the disparity between the rich and poor are more visible on the streets than they have been in the past forty years, the city has seen an uptick in popularity — the same week we moved in, our movers transported three new families to the area — and house prices have skyrocketed.

The number at the women's shelter rings and rings until the answering machine picks up. I call again. No answer.

A middle-aged white man stops at the light and he's staring at me like he has something to say. I lower the phone from my ear and call out to him.

"That's all this town is now," he says, shaking his head in disapproval. "It's full of them."

I understand he is referencing homelessness, drug addiction, but I don't see how this is supposed to help me or this woman by my side, in crisis.

"It's okay — you can go," the woman says to me at one point, half-heartedly releasing me. But her need lies before me like a well gone dry, while I have water to spare. *Water that is older than the sun. Water that remembers where we came from.*

I dial again. The voice on the answering machine at the women's shelter says they may be on the other line or busy with a client. I call again and again. No answer.

The woman stumbles back into a fold-out chair placed casually against the brick wall of the convenience store. The store clerk emerges in his button-down shirt. He gives me a weak, nervous smile, then glances in the direction of the woman, then disappears back inside. The woman is holding herself, loosely, and I notice her eyes are mostly closed and she's fighting to stay awake.

"I just need to sleep," she says.

No answer at the shelter. The answering machine gives the number for an emergency crisis line, and I finally decide to call it. I look to the girls: "Remember this! Nine-five-six," I say to one girl. "Nine-seven-eight-five," I say to the other.

They stand there, repeating their respective numbers under their breaths like a mantra, like a woman's life depends on it.

I call the first three digits, then point to each of them in turn and they dole out their numbers like good girls.

While the phone is ringing, I finally think to ask the woman for her name.

Her voice is like a whisper, and I can't hear her the first time. The third try is clear: "Cassy."

Cassy, okay. I'm going to find you a shelter, Cassy. A place to rest. All she needs for now is a place to rest. Cassy is sleeping upright in the fold-out chair.

I finally get through to someone at the crisis line and explain the situation. Corner of Hunter and Aylmer. Woman in distress who needs shelter. Can someone come and pick her up?

Does she qualify for a youth shelter? The crisis worker wants to know. This may help.

"How old are you?" I ask Cassy.

Eyes closed, she answers. "Twenty-eight." Pain written across her face.

"Is she hurt? In need of medical attention?" the crisis operator asks.

This is a hard question for me to answer. There are no obvious gaping wounds — but then, aren't there?

"Are you hurt, Cassy?" I ask.

"Yea, I'm hurt," she says. "I've been raped my whole life. And it hurts. It hurts." A few tears squeeze from her eyes down her mottled cheeks.

Did I repeat those words? *She's been raped her whole life.* Or did the operator hear her clearly across the line — I can't remember.

"Girls, go over and see if the café is open." I send them down the street and they stand there, peering into the closed dessert shop, hands cupped against the glass, giving us space and finding a place for themselves to breathe.

A grey-bearded man who embodies the unkempt appearance of the homeless approaches Cassy at this moment. He doesn't connect with me, but moves right to her, gently shaking her folded arms. "You gotta wake up, man, you gotta wake up."

Cassy doesn't stir, and the man moves on quickly, head down, slouched shoulders.

The crisis operator is sympathetic, but there is not much she can say or do from where she's sitting. She gives me a hazy location for the shelter, which is much, much too far for Cassy to walk in her current state, but doable for someone who would fill out work-out pants like the ones falling off her hips. Only one other option remains.

"All you can do," the crisis worker informs me, "is call the nonemergency police line. They'll be able to help her."

I have a feeling that isn't going to sit well with Cassy.

I hang up and tell Cassy the bad news.

"Cassy, what do you think about me calling the nonemergency police to come and take you to the shelter?"

"No, no," she says, "they hurt me." She tries to stand up, but I gently block her path, ask her to wait. She stumbles back down into the chair anyway.

"I promise I will stay with you and talk to them. It'll be okay." But I don't know that things will be okay for her. I say this on behalf of myself. For her, how things will end up, I have no idea. How could I imagine what her life is like? We are distant stars, light years apart. What I meant, then, is that the police will make things okay for me, the law-abiding citizen.

Even so, I really don't want to call the police; to do so feels like a betrayal to Cassy. I want to help her. I'm not sure whether calling the police will help. I know it will be a young male police officer who will show up. How could he possibly understand what a woman who's been raped her whole life and is addicted to drugs has been through? Are male police officers trained in trauma and crisis management and women's mental health with more than a passing glance, more than a cursory course or a chapter in a textbook? I have a feeling that's not what draws most young men into police work.

I feel deeply for this woman. Will they hurt her? She says they will because experience has taught her; they have in the past. When we don't trust someone, does that make them more dangerous?

I call the nonemergency police. What choice do I have? The girls are still standing near the closed dessert shop. The operator who answers asks for my name and location, and a physical description of the woman.

"What's her name?" she wants to know.

"Cassy."

"Okay, I've got an officer in the area — he'll be right over."

"Wait," I say. "Will they help her? I mean, can they take her to a shelter?"

She says something about the officers assessing the situation and if there's space, and if Cassy qualifies under some set of criteria unknown to me, that yes, she will be given a ride to the shelter.

I can't imagine a world where she doesn't qualify. And if she doesn't, who does?

"Okay, should I stay with her until the officer arrives?"

"That's up to you," the operator says matter-of-factly.

I'm not going anywhere.

A minute later, a man's voice from behind startles me.

"Hey, Cass, how are you today?" The young police officer approaches, hands on his hips, like a reprimanding parent. "You on anything?"

Eyes wide, she stands up, slouching, then gesticulates, hands in motion.

"It's okay — you can go," he says to me off to the side, conspiratorially, like I am released.

But I don't move, can't move. My feet know to stay.

"It's just—" I say, and now I have his full attention. "She said she's tired. She needs a place to sleep. Can you take her to the women's shelter?"

"We'll take care of her, don't worry," he says. And there's no malice in his voice. No intent to hurt. No intent to hurt, but I cannot tell, I cannot ascertain from this passing interaction, if there is an intent to heal.

❋

Standing inside Freshii, the girls by my side, our order placed, I see two police cruisers drive away. I strain to see inside the back of the first vehicle and think I spot a slouched figure, but I can't be sure. A quick glance over at the convenience store reveals the corner is empty, abandoned. Does transporting Cassy to the women's shelter down the street really require two police cruisers? By the time our food arrives and I pull out of the parking lot with the girls in tow, the same two police cruisers pull up beside me with their back seats empty. No passengers inside. Why do I feel then that what I've done is criminal, when I'm the one standing on the outside?

I think about Cassy on the drive up to the cottage and find I can't eat. What will Cassy be eating for dinner, if anything? I thought about how I was loved and cared for as a child, how she was degraded and raped, and how that set us both up for different paths in life. I kept focusing on how Cassy's life could have been my life, if the circumstances were different, reversed. If circumstances were different. We might not be here at all if it weren't for a handful of exploding stars.

When I tell my husband about what happened, he has a slightly different take.

"She could never imagine what your life must be like," he says.

But I think he's got it wrong.

"We are all more blind to what we have than to what we have not,"[8] Audre Lorde wrote on a trip to Russia. And what I have is guilt. Guilt that I am free in ways that Cassy is not, may never be. Guilt that some people shine bright, while others burn. Guilt for the ones I can't save and guilt for wanting to save them — or not. And because *it could have been me*. I, too, come from a supernova. I, too, could collapse under the heft of my own weight. Only a thin sheath exists between us — lines that aren't even real.

"We are dead stars," astronomer Michelle Thaller observed, "looking back up at the sky."[9] Looking back up at ourselves.

And maybe it was that in looking back at Cassy, I could see myself. A painful reminder: we are pieces of broken stars.

✳

Cassy visited me in a dream a few nights later. She looked beautiful — of course she did. Skin clear, healthy and flushed. Eyes bright;
dark, thick lashes; an ethereal gown. She seemed to know where I
was and had decided to come visit me at the cottage.

"It's nice," she said, "your life."

She looked well, safe, and happy. I hugged her.

But it was only a dream.

Author's Note

Several months after I encountered Cassy, I attended a yoga retreat
with a group of local women. Two of the women worked downtown, and I overheard them saying a homeless woman they both
knew had died.

Goosebumps trailed down my spine and a stone landed in my
stomach. "Do you have a picture?"

We found her on Facebook. Or Cassy had again found me. A
newspaper article[10] detailed the tragic ending of her life. She had
been diagnosed with schizophrenia in high school and faced other
mental health challenges. She was unable to get help, which led to
street drugs to self-medicate, addiction, and homelessness. She had
lost a child.

Shortly after I met her, Cassy disappeared, and her family
marked her as missing. Police investigations revealed she was kid-
napped and sold into the sex trade in Toronto, but after thirty days
she somehow escaped, made her way back to town. Cassy had a
"hellish life" (according to her mom), but she was loved. Her body
was found behind a dumpster on September 20, 2021. She died
from suspected opioid poisoning.

Cassy was still alive when I encountered her in my dream.

I connected with Cassy's family after the retreat, and they gave me permission to share her story and her real name: Cassandra (a.k.a. Cassy) Alexandre, in the hope that her story will inspire change for those with mental health challenges. In the hope that she has not died in vain. Rest in peace, Cassy.

Cepheid: An Astronomy of Female Friendship

ONE STARRY AUGUST night, as teen girls, we camped overnight in my friend Megan's unfenced backyard, the moon tucked just outside the flaps of our tent. Megs, as I called her then, lived in a suburban neighbourhood, a ridiculous place to camp, and yet there we were, four girls in her backyard, exposed to passersby, spending the night outside like her cats.

In the morning, sun filtered through the canvas and reached our drowsy eyes. I fought to hold onto sleep and my friends turned on me with crazed expressions as they pinned me to the ground and tickled my sides until I thought I would burst.

Megs was the one to show me mercy. "Okay, she's had enough, let her go." Their love and attention, the strength of our bond, filled me.

We lazed around and talked until dark clouds threatened, then we packed up the tent and moved indoors. We had no responsibilities, nothing we were expected to do that day. As the rain poured through the heat of the afternoon, we couldn't resist the draw and ran out in our two-piece bathing suits. We laughed and rejoiced as the wet warmth coated our skin, filled our noses, soaked our hair and bodies. We ran around Megs's yard in our bare feet, mushy grass between our toes, then stomped through puddles in the middle of the paved road. We whooped and threw our arms upward in a state of euphoric, raw delight.

In an instant, the heavy downpour slowed and then stopped. The air crackled. We stood spread out, in silence, and listened while the sky sparked. Lightning touched down, striking a hill in the distance. We counted the seconds after the flash, and in the next breath came the loud thunder *BOOM* and we screamed. We fled in the direction of the house but stopped ourselves as the sun slid partially into the sky and the hush returned. Oversized droplets fell intermittently. I looked over my shoulder at Megs, who pointed to the clouds: "Look!" A massive rainbow hung in the parting shadows, its colours enveloping the sky.

We screamed some more, gleeful about the rainbow, grasped each other's soaked palms, ran holding hands, and jumped in the puddles. The four of us threw our arms around each other's misty bodies; in that embrace, we connected in a way that left me electrically charged and tethered to the earth. I didn't want to let go. I held tight to my friends, whose camaraderie made me insanely happy.

A Cepheid (pronounced SEE + FEE + ID), also known as a Cepheid variable, is a type of supergiant star that brightens and dims periodically.[1] These stars pulsate outward and are among the brightest in the sky, especially at their peak. Is female friendship like this, brightening and dimming over time? Cepheid variable stars, along with supernovas, can be used to measure vast intergalactic distances, such as the span between galaxies. At the height of their luminosity, Cepheids are forty thousand times brighter than the sun.[2]

The more massive the star, the more luminous.[3] In girlhood, my female friendships shone as some of the brightest stars in the sky — but what about in womanhood? What happens to female friendship as a girl matures, if she chooses to marry and then become a mother, as I did?

*

Megs and I didn't begin as friends. In grade one, we fought over whose hair was longer, longest.

"Mine is!"

"No mine is!"

The rivalry continued. Her golden pigtails stretched down to her waist and were longer than mine, but I would never admit it.

In grade six, she was a competitive figure skater; I was a competitive gymnast.

Megan talked about her gruelling off-ice training.

"Gymnastics requires the most skill," I retorted. "I heard it on the radio." I couldn't resist getting the last word.

Megs shrugged, indifferent.

She's such a snob, I thought.

By the end of elementary school, we had evolved beyond hair dramatics and competition over whose sport was tougher, drawing nearer one another, orbiting closer, helio-adolescents, pulled into the same sunny group of friends.

That summer, on the cusp of high school and womanhood, four of us were at a friend's cottage.

We dived off the dock and swam to Seagull Poop Island — a formation of shit-covered rocks we had named and claimed as our own.

Megs and I sunned ourselves on the rocks, wearing matching halter-top bikinis. She reached her arms over the back of her head as she interweaved the three strands of hair to create her own French braid.

"How do you do that?" I asked.

"Easy — I can teach you. Want me to do yours?"

I left the braid in for the rest of the weekend.

I had believed Megs to be one thing, but from a slightly different angle, I could see she was someone other completely, whose glittery pieces shone multidirectionally. I recognized myself in her refracted light, and together, we shone brighter.

In her family, Megs was the long-awaited daughter: the fourth child, the only girl, following three brothers. She was comfortable around boys. She went mountain biking, often getting ejected from her seat, with one of the guys in her neighbourhood who would eventually become my boyfriend.

✶

At the end of high school, we were a handful of couples sleeping at Megs's cottage. That night, after we had drunk, swum, drunk and played cards, drunk and played board games, we coupled off into our respective rooms for bed and I fought with my then-boyfriend. I was furious at him for ignoring me. I claimed his attention was directed elsewhere. I hissed at him, in an angry whisper, "You spent more time talking to *Megan* than you did talking to *me*."

The next morning was awkward.

"Everyone could hear you last night," Megs said to me at the breakfast table, exasperated. "The walls are paper thin! What did you think would happen?"

Years later, when I broke up with the boyfriend, Megs told me she had met up with him — only once. They had gone mountain biking together. "He's doing okay," she told me, because she knew I needed to know.

✶

The first time Megs invited me to her cottage, we were sixteen and swimming in her lake when I spotted a creature nearby. "Megs, Megs! Look!"

Shhh! She held a finger to her lips. "Loons are shy birds," she told me. "We don't want to scare him away."

We swam over to the dock, and she showed me how to imitate the regal bird's tremolo. "Cup your hands, like this." And she clasped one hand on top of the other, as though sheltering a baby bird or a lit candle. "Put your thumbs together, but leave a little space for air to get in. Rest your lips on your knuckles — yep," she helped me adjust my grip, "and whistle like this."

She blew and blew into her cupped palms, until the stream of air became flute-like, avian.

A second loon landed nearby and we squealed silently.

I spent the rest of the weekend perfecting my imitative pitch, blowing warm air into my palms until I heard the loon's call echo from my hands to the far horizon of the lake. I will teach this skill to my own daughters, the sleight of hand, a reverberation of friendship, that embeds itself into memory like the night's twinkling sky.

*

In high school, I read *Seventeen* magazine and filled out one of those questionnaires designed to reveal something mind-blowing about the relationships in my life. In the blank spaces, I recorded names in response to questions like: *Who do you tell your deepest secrets to? Who do you go to when you have a problem?* My answers revealed my best friend, my (not-so-) secret crush, and another category akin to soulmate, which I hadn't anticipated. Megan's name landed in the spot for "this person is your lucky star." Those two words felt particularly true, and I held onto them even as the years dilated and the black matter between us expanded.

＊

According to NASA, Cepheid variables are a special class of star because the rate at which their light rises and falls can be related to their intrinsic brightness. Intrinsic brightness is a star's true luminosity, its real shine. What we see from Earth is a star's apparent brightness. By comparing intrinsic and apparent brightness, astronomers can use Cepheid variable stars to make reliable measurements of large cosmic distances.[4] Cepheids as cosmic yardsticks.

I believed that the brightness of our friendships, the one I had with Megan and my other girlfriends, would never go away. That I could carry the luminosity of such relationships throughout my life and that the brightness of our bonds would hold steady. Because how could I let this brilliance, at its most luminous forty thousand times brighter than the sun, ever fade?

The connection I feel to other women is a yardstick for my happiness.

A Cepheid variable loses its reliability as a cosmic yardstick if some of its light is absorbed on the way to Earth, by intervening dust. Dust absorbs light, making the star appear fainter and farther away than it really is.[5]

＊

Megs and I attended different universities, moved to different cities, and grew into adulthood, though we stayed in touch. Somewhere in the intervening years, in the dust of marriage and motherhood and disability parenting, the intensity and light of our friendship faded, was absorbed, reduced to a faint flicker, a dimness, over physical distance and time.

When Elyse was born with Down syndrome, I found myself in a new galaxy. Some friendships brightened while others dimmed.

The baby needed surgery, and we were weeks in hospital. Megs and my other school friends donated to the Canadian Down Syndrome Society on our baby's behalf, which meant something. I pumped breast milk eight times a day, through the night, and listened to Bruno Mars croon on the radio on my daily drive to the hospital in between visits with Ariel at home. I sat in a wipeable chair, staring at my baby under her glass case. My only priority was family. That our baby should live. The hospital time was a black hole and Megs remained somewhere on the other side.

Once the baby was home, my days were full caring for a toddler and a baby, forty-five-minute drives to speech therapy sessions, potty training, developmental support worker appointments, library storytime, occupational therapy, two dogs to walk, a husband absent for work. But on one precious occasion, Meg and I held space for each other.

✹

Cepheid stars oscillate between two states: compact and expanded. When the star is compact, large temperature and pressure gradients build up, which gradually causes the star to expand. In its expanded state, the star eventually succumbs to the forces of gravity and contracts back to its shrunken state.[6] I picture the Cepheid star breathing in, lungs expanded, holding its shimmery breath — the way I held certain aspects of myself in as a young mother — then release, breathing out, deflating. The relief of unloading that mounting pressure.

✹

Now in our mid-thirties, Megan exits her cottage bedroom. I have only Penelope with me and Meg has both of her children. Our combined three kids are finally asleep. The cottage is dimly lit, cozy, and mostly contained to one room, with bedrooms shooting off the side and an additional sunken, screened-in porch. The worn couches, chairs, and décor scream seventies, and a musky, dust-laden odour mixes with the surrounding pines. We are two women, alone, with our three sleeping children, nestled into a forest in a cottage accessible only by boat. Bears arrive regularly at the screen door beside the kitchen, attracted by the smell of BBQ cooking. With dark night encroaching, bears may lurk in the back of my mind, but what I want more than anything is to cool off in the lake.

I am anxious to escape the oppressive, muggy heat of the cottage. To step out into the night air and set free the animal moisture dousing my skin. The two of us have set up camp, entertained with toys, prepared the dinner, fed the babies, cleaned the mess of spaghetti strands off the faces and floors and table and chairs. We have brushed teeth with bottled water, read storybooks, nursed, and snuggled in tight until droopy eyelids closed. We have done it all, except the one thing I want most. We arrived at the cottage earlier in the day and yet still have not gone swimming. We may have splashed around on a foam mat, but the water is too deep to stand on the bottom and we are outnumbered. I am dying to go swimming with my friend. So much of motherhood is about patience, about putting your kids' needs first and waiting to fulfill your own needs. Meg and I could have traded off, watched each other's babies in the cottage, but we don't want to spend time apart and neither one of us wants to do that to the other — the added responsibility.

With the children tentatively asleep, eagerness written onto my face, a conspiratorial glance from her, I know I want to swim but I'm unsure what my friend will propose. With the passage of time, we remain close, but who she is in her daily life is a mystery to me now.

"Skinny dipping," she offers. "It's a cottage tradition — do you want to?"

One leg is already out of my pants.

We turn away to give each other privacy, modest in our motherhood bodies and lactating chests. Even in motherhood, my friend remains a slender beauty; she glows, forehead high, and pearl coloured as a full moon, under her towel.

We stand there a moment, on the precipice of leaving, clutching our towels. A distant rumble from the sky's belly comes from outside. The pressure and temperature inside me are building: time to expand to our brightest true selves.

Meg glances in the direction of the sleeping children. "We won't be long," she whispers.

Is this promised assurance for the children or for herself or for my benefit? I'm not entirely sure.

Our motherly charge is to watch over these sleeping beings, who will summon and rouse us both in the night for sustenance, little hungry werewolves called by the moon. But in this moment after their last feeding, milk-drunk and passed out, we mothers are finally free.

What strikes me now is for how little time we left them — five minutes? — before we towelled off, climbed back up those slippery steps, got our own jammies on, and collapsed into our respective beds with exhaustion. We allowed ourselves just one jump. It had to be a good jump, the best jump there ever was — a jump that would serve as our last for a long while.

"Hold my hand," Meg whispers, towels wrapped tight around our torsos.

I take my friend's hand as she reaches for the screen door.

"The rocks are slippery at night."

We are both giddy, me at the thought of leaving the children behind, of cooling warm flesh outdoors and plunging off the dock.

I sense Meg is enjoying sharing this part of her world with her long-time friend; of being my guiding light in the darkness.

Her hand grasped in mine, suddenly I am fourteen again, running toward the thunderstorm. I giggle as the door creaks and my free hand flies up to cover my mouth, like we are having a sleepover and staying up past our bedtime and her parents might hear us. Meg's finger hovers at her lips, eyes wide, a soothing *shhh* with a smile across her lips. Ah, so we are both yearning for this reprieve. We must not mess it up — if one of the babies should wake …

We slip into the night, darkness complete, under a parabola of stars and skip down the stairs of the poorly lit path in the hill that leads to the wooden dock. The air is thick with a coolness rushing in. I say skip, but we are running, away from responsibility and nursing babies and our husbands' needs and every stifling aspect of motherhood and wifedom. The constant devotion and eclipsing of oneself, hiding in the shadows, somewhere on the other side. *Here you are*, I think of my friend in that moment, *I have you. The* real *you, childhood Megan.* The friend who would argue with me over whose hair is longer. Those days, a luxury. A mother's time is hardly ever her own.

"Want to hold hands when we jump?" Meg asks at normal volume, excitement in her voice — she's daring me — as we gain distance from the cottage.

The last few steps, we fly toward the water with the exhilaration of breaking free. My feet don't touch the ground.

The thought of holding hands while jumping into the lake freaks me out, but I trust Megan. I know she will know when it is time to let go.

Besides, there's no time to argue with her. We drop our towels in unison on the dock and fling ourselves over the edge, toward the black water, letting out a scream at the cold shock.

Somewhere mid-air, entering the depths, Megan lets go, and I submerge completely into the deep.

I come up immediately, searching for breath, laughing, and treading water next to my friend, her eyes two glowing crescents. I peer back toward the dock at the dark treeline of forest, the lit cottage, and the full, low-hanging moon nestled above our sleeping babies. Momentarily, treading water alongside Meg, I feel safe and familiar. Joy rises inside me. In this reclamation of girlhood, I feel wholly, completely myself. *Here I am.* And I know both what I have lost, and what I will always hold onto. Even if only for a short while.

The moment passes quickly. Clouds crowd in and the sky tears open. The downpour arrives to break the oppressive heat.

Meg and I scramble up the ladder, back onto the dock, fumble for our towels as our teeth chatter in the cold rain and refreshing night air. We cackle at the rain, the idea of fish caressing our exposed breasts, and was that seaweed that touched my arm? We are incandescent celestial bodies at our brightest point, forty thousand times brighter than the sun.

We hurry, together, back up the steps.

Aporia

I AM THE one pretending like I don't know what it is I want to do.

My first career was as a classroom teacher. At twenty-four years old, I was in charge of the French education of twenty-three six-year-olds. At the end of my second year of teaching, I became a mother, something other.

I leaned into pregnancy and parenthood with the same gusto with which I had once wanted to teach. Motherhood chose me. The pull was internal, complete. I knew exactly what I wanted: a baby to fit perfectly into the crook of my arm in the grocery store aisles. A baby to push in the stroller alongside winding rivers, under blue cloud-dotted skies, down willow tree paths. A baby to pull from my milky breasts, engorged to full moons. A baby to sing stories to and dream in lullabies. A baby to *coo coo* and keep me company in the night. A baby to love so fully, the moon would hover close by my window to gaze at the sight. A beloved pet. I was enamoured with the idea of motherhood. The reality was perhaps a titch more fraught, but no less filled with love that is both jagged and smooth.

The first pregnancy took like a haunting; I was with child before you could say *boo*. I wanted each of my babies badly. I also wanted to maintain some semblance of self.

Is it a privilege to want children and get them? Is it always a privilege, as a woman, to want something and be allowed to have it? What if wanting something precludes me from having it? If the wanting keeps me from the having? What if we want two things and those two things are in direct conflict with one another? I have the things I want; shouldn't that be enough to keep me satisfied? Shouldn't I just be grateful for my children, to be a mother — isn't that enough?

Is it enough for a father?

Have you seen a fire catch? The unmistakable shift; the amber flames licking at the wood ferociously, a heat that lasts all day. I want to burn as brightly and with such a ferocity as to surprise, amaze — delight. But I'm afraid I'm like a lit piece of paper, all flash and screaming flame, quick to burn out, not one that endures or has any real substance. The pretense of a real fire.

I am the one pretending like I don't know what it is I want to do. Why the need to pretend?

To protect myself.

　　　　　　　　　　　　　✷

I raised three daughters and had at least one child at home for almost a decade. During that time, I was primarily responsible for their care.

"This is all you have to do today," I reminded myself lovingly, at first, when babies wouldn't sleep, and the dishes piled up, and my husband travelled for work for weeks at a time, and grandparents dropped by, and playdates were expected, and the dog needed walking, and no sleep was to be had, not a wink. *This is all you have to do today.* The words were meant as reassurance. It was okay to let go of my outer ambitions and fall headlong into the demands of motherhood. I would find my way back to a career. *No big deal.* Years would tick by. *No. Big. Deal.* I wasn't lost, I was just ... elsewhere. The thing with motherhood, though, is that it's permanent.

I wouldn't trade the formative years I spent with my children for a career or some other version of a life. The intimacy of being the one there to experience their growth and look after my family was worth it to me. I believe in the minute, intimate moments of the domestic — their grandness — and I also understand how debasing and destabilizing parenting can be. And consuming.

My husband's career climbs at a clever, stable diagonal, and I'm grateful to him for that stability and his sacrifices and commitment to our family. But he will never know what it means to have a work life interrupted. I could not have imagined what beginning again would feel like, the sense of invisibility — and how hard I would have to work to be seen as anything other than a mother.

I am the one pretending like I don't know what it is I want to do. Why the need to pretend? To be perceived as a devoted, good mother.

I became a writer after Elyse was born as a way to advocate on her behalf. This is the story I told myself and the one that I've told to others, over and over, about why I write. Writing as a way to advocate for my daughter with Down syndrome. But this is only a partial truth. Writing is also a way to advocate for myself. The narrative of the altruistic mother is one others can readily accept; it's the story where I am the least selfish, where I shine in the best possible light. It's the story that grants me permission.

Teaching is an acceptable profession for a woman, as is being a mother — but writing? Pursuing the arts? What I viewed as sustaining — necessary — others considered self-indulgent. Even as I pursued writing, I felt the need to pretend that motherhood remained my top priority.

Writing happened under black skies, holed up in cafés with an unplugged laptop. I kept a notebook in my purse to catch dispatches as they came on the way to nursery storytime, mad scribbles at red lights in the car. Writing happened during naptime — if I didn't also fall asleep. Writing happened when I signed up my tots for half-day preschool a few days a week. I squeezed out all the emotion I could onto the page in one- or two-hour stretches. When preschool switched to a few full days for Elyse, and Ariel was in kindergarten, I wrote fiendishly in the five- or six-hour window, then I'd wipe my eyes dry before picking them up. I was drafting a complete memoir, reading religiously, and teaching myself to write. But because I wasn't making an income, my labour was meaningless to the outside world.

What do you do?

"I'm a teacher, but now I'm home with my kids," I used to say, even though by that point I couldn't imagine going back to elementary school teaching with my two, then three, kids in the primary age bracket.

Over time, my story changed. "I used to be a teacher," I could admit, "but now I'm home with my kids and I'm writing a book." I didn't want it to look like I was freeloading off my husband. I was the one who earned money first, while Dan finished his Ph.D., and I was the one who had made the down payment on our home. But regardless of my financial contributions and the immense unpaid labour that is full-time child care, I was still a freeloader, and possibly also a fake, according to some comments.

A neighbour who read the first newspaper article I published leaned over the fence between our yards and complimented me on the piece.

Then she said, "But Dan must have written that?"

No, I corrected her, he hadn't.

"But he helped you, then?"

✦

If I pretend to be uncertain about writing for the sake of look-ing like a better, more devoted mother, then I'm equally uncertain about my devotion to motherhood. But it's a pretend uncertainty.

I am the one pretending like I don't know what it is I want to do.
What I want to do is light a fire.

For whom does the fire burn, if not for the ones we love? Nothing makes me feel like more of a fraud in my own life than the ones I love, than the ones who truly see me.

I arrange logs in our firepit at the cottage. Why am I doing what I'm doing? I'm building the fire because I want to look to my husband like a good mother and a capable and competent outdoors-woman in front of my children. I'm building the fire because I want to eat s'mores with the kids, because it's better for the environment, because I feel compelled to do so at this time. I'm building the fire because I want to. Which is the truest response? Do my motivations truly define my behaviour, more so than the behaviour itself? Does whether I want to light the fire matter, if it is my children who want me to do so? If it is my husband who asks it of me? Or if it is be-cause I want it most? The answer makes me sick. I will pretend I'm building the fire for my family's benefit instead of my own because selflessness is what's expected of me. I'm resentful of my status as a woman; as a mother; as one who must cater to others. Do men cater to the needs of others the way women do? I don't think so. They burn for the sake of their own wood.

✦

The sun rises, a golden curtain blanketing the sky. I'm at the cottage of my friend Amy and her husband, Mike, with my two older girls, and it's summertime — first light. I'm standing in the kitchen, looking longingly out at the lake. I want to go for a swim, but nothing is ever that simple when you're responsible for children.

My friends are just waking up. I hear heavy footsteps coming down the hallway from the back of the cottage, where Mike and Amy sleep in the new addition Mike has built onto the original cottage. The footfall peters out into the bathroom. I hear the unmistakable arc of piss hitting its target and the whoosh from the bucket of water to wash the urine away. The cottage has no running water — a project for a later date.

Mike himself emerges, shirtless, spackle in hand, hair twisted up in a cowlick of sleep. He is quiet, understated and, as such, I jokingly refer to him as "Magic Mike," riffing off the movie whose main character is a male stripper. Mike stays fit through manual labour and used to work as a bartender in our high school days, at a bar called The Rooster. In French, a rooster is *un coq* (the rooster. Cock. Get it?). Unlike in the movie, I've never seen our Mike jump onto the bar top, taking swigs of tequila, arms around scantily clad women, swinging his shirt over his head, thrusting his manly bits. No, that version of Mike is only in the movies; the Mike I know is a dad. He's shy, yet sure of himself in a way that arouses envy.

Before Mike drinks a drop of coffee or eats a bite of breakfast, he begins spackling the new cottage walls he's recently erected. He is smoothing a surface in preparation for decoration, paint. I watch him and appreciate his passion for his craft; in his actions, I recognize an identical passion for mine. My urge to write is equally as strong as Mike's urge to spackle; we are both makers. But there's something more. I want what he has, the ease with which he is able to fully inhabit himself, without barriers. His wife, my friend Amy, has by now gotten the coffee brewed, and without breaking his stride Mike takes a steaming hot mug from her in his free hand and continues spackling with the other. *I want that*, I think. What I see, what I want, is his freedom. The ease with which he is settled into his own bones. The ease with which he goes about his work uninhibited.

In contrast, my own movements to get to the page are restrained and hampered by invisible handcuffs. My passion is illicit, time to engage in my craft stolen. Back then, I didn't yet consider myself a Real Writer, and until I could somehow prove that I was, art-making needed to happen outside of motherhood's all-consuming business hours. Special dates were arranged for me to visit Starbucks in the evening once the kids were asleep, and in the beginning, especially, these dates with myself felt like moving the prime minister. Writing was viewed as indulgent, me-time, not the direction I was steering my career. Writing was something to be earned once my other responsibilities were tended to, like if I collected enough motherhood gold stars, I could cash in. In other words, I am the one pouring the coffee, not drinking it while typing on my keyboard.

What I see in Mike's way of being is what I want as a writer. To move unfettered through the world. To own a task and know it is yours for the doing. To be free to write when I want and when I determine I need to. Not as an afterthought or as self-care or in the after-hours. To see passion so clearly in another, I cannot unsee it in myself as an artist. "It was less like seeing than like being for the first time seen, knocked breathless by a powerful glance," Annie Dillard wrote in her essay "Seeing." "Gradually the lights went out in the cedar, the colors died, the cells unflamed and disappeared. I was still ringing. I had been my whole life a bell, and never knew it until at that moment I was lifted and struck."[1] This is what it is for me to inhabit my body fully as a writer; I experience the ringing, tucked away on those café chairs, writing. Why is it so hard to admit what I want, which is to write, unencumbered? To piss in the pot, pick up my pen, and go to it. Why do I hold in my urge to spackle like a secret shame? I've been ringing and ringing like a doorbell, but many times have had to pretend like there's nobody home.

If I admit what I want and I don't get it, then I will be crushed. What if I take the spackle from my husband's hand, say "it's my turn," and he says "no." Then what?

And even if Dan does give me exactly what I want, time and space — which is what he will eventually do — then I have to contend with the very real possibility that I could fail, as a writer. I could very well fail. Others could perceive my thoughts and ideas as no good, of little worth, of no value. Useless. Or worse. Nobody could care at all. If you ring a bell, and there's no one there to hear it, does it make a sound?

The perfectionist in me cares too much about what other people think.

What if I'm like a nesting doll of phony layers? Peel back the shiny, smiling facade and at the centre you'll find the hard little woman who may or may not be of substance; she sure isn't taking up room. Likely, she is hollow. This is my greatest fear with self-expression. But there's more. I can't just pick up the nails and start hammering walls together when women are expected to be painted and delicate, as light as air; to be multifaceted, yet identical and uni-purpose. What holds me back, beyond my own self-doubt as a writer, in other words, is that I am expected to be a certain kind of mother. The kind who puts the needs of her children before herself.

But what if I don't want to be that kind of mother anymore?

✳

I am the one pretending like I don't know what it is I want to do. Why the need to pretend? I can't be both fully devoted to motherhood and fully devoted to writing. I will always be split between the two.

✳

A few years after my visit to Amy and Mike's cottage, I sit in the summer sun on my own dock, reading Bahar Orang's *Where Things Touch: A Meditation on Beauty*. Several pages in, I notice the word "aporia." *What a beautiful word*, I think. *What does it mean?* Here is the context in which it appears in Orang's work:

> Perhaps my writing, here, is the articulation of a series of ruptures — all the times I appeared to be waiting but was actually searching. My search has changed, though, because I hardly know anymore whether I can even articulate that aporia that is beauty, or if it even wishes to be expressed at all.[2]

An aporia is a rhetorical device that expresses uncertainty or doubt, often pretend uncertainty or doubt about something; it is an irresolvable internal contradiction or logical disjunction in a text, argument, or theory. Elizabeth Barrett Browning's "Sonnet 43" — the poem my sister-in-law Medrie read at our wedding — is one example of aporia. Browning's words of love are an expression of insincere doubt. "How do I love thee? Let me count the ways ... I love thee to the level of every day's / Most quiet need."[3] Asking the question allows her to enumerate an answer and emphasize her point.

By not claiming space for my art, I am the aporia, the one feigning uncertainty, the one who pretends to others like I don't know what it is I want to do.

✳

On the day of my arrival at Mike and Amy's cottage, I spot Mike outside, kneeling down low beside my eldest daughter. Eight years old and Ariel's got a drill and a nail in hand, and Mike is teaching her how to use them. Mike's day job is as a high school tech teacher.

He's patient with my daughter, kind. He makes sure that each kid, my two and his two, get their fair share of turns with the drill, including Elyse, who is six. Together, they build a new deck in half a day's time. Mike's way of caring for the children is to include them. None of us are in the way when we have a job to do. Can I have this? Can I find a way to merge time with my daughters into my writing life?

✴

Eleven years into being a writer and five years from that moment when I saw Mike get up and spackle, I tell my youngest daughter bedtime stories and record them on my iPhone. We attend a book launch in a museum. We write surrealist kid poems at bedtime, involving giant talking cupcakes and octopuses and blue foxes and mermaid twins. My eldest, now twelve, is travelling to Greece with me, on a writing retreat self-funded by my earnings as a writer. We go out as a family to a tacky restaurant to celebrate my hundredth rejection. I have found ways for my children and family to be interwoven into the fabric of my writing life.

The fire inside me burns bright because of my love for my children. I want them to understand what it means to live a fulfilling life. But the sensation of the bell ringing? That deep knowing of who I am, and understanding that "writer" is one of my many callings in life? That's me. That's who I've always been.

✴

I come across a journal entry I wrote on summer vacation, when I was a childless classroom teacher. "I'm going to write a book." Those words are inked on the page. "But I don't know about what." My creative life has exploded into my motherhood life, and vice versa. The two lives are intertwined, and both are essential to my identity. I continue to fight for a balance between home and work, careful not to let one or the other consume me. And I don't have to pretend anymore. I don't have to pretend like I don't know what it is I want to do.

My alarm clock goes off at six a.m. When my husband is home, which is often enough, he prepares the girls' breakfasts and packs their lunches for school. The dog follows me as I lace up my running shoes or stretch in yoga poses. I don't feel the need to begin with writing every day, but the choice is mine. Often, I channel my inner Mike. I get up, piss in the pot, sit down at the keyboard in my small office right away. I insist on making my own tea, the way I like it. And I write.

I visit my cottage for writing residencies of my own creation. The sun wavers in the sky, says her final goodbye. I perch myself at the end of the dock and listen to the loons' hollow calls echo as the sun winds down and carves a shimmering path along the water to my feet. I write, *When the lake laughs, the waves catch the sunlight like cupped hands.* I think I'll stay by the shore a while with my notebook, pen poised in hand, see what else comes up. I will give myself the gift of time to continue unravelling the messy yarn of my life. To follow the golden thread, as William Stafford called it. I will follow the golden thread, walk along new trails, step deep into the woods, and listen for porcupines. Pause my footsteps, attend. To paraphrase Mary Oliver, what better use of my time could there possibly be?[4] The sun slips below the dark horizon of the hills. Maybe the thread will pull back in a new direction, away from the forest, the dock, toward the podium of another dream. I'll still be a mother. Always a mother. But also something other.

The Best Fortune

IN 2019, IN the land of the rising sun, travelling by shinkansen from Hiroshima to Kyoto, eight-year-old Ariel removes her favourite pink sweatshirt. When our family of five disembarks, the sweatshirt is accidentally left behind on the train seat.

★

Four years later, I sit at my writing desk, laptop open to Google Search, and type in "coin flip." I arbitrarily assign "heads" to mean "yes" and "tails" to mean "no." I click the touch pad to flip the coin and ask question after question. I record each coin-flip answer dictated by chance. What follows are not my chosen responses, but rather the answers given to me by random coin flips, which have allowed me to listen more deeply to what only I need to hear.

> *Should I go to California again? Yes.*
> *Thailand? Yes.*
> *Hawaii? Yes.*

Japan? No.
Oops, I forgot Portugal. Should I go to Portugal
again? No.
Will this make it into my book? Yes.

I attend a Sheila Heti workshop and she encourages us to use coin flipping to help make tough decisions pertaining to our life and particularly our writing life, in regular intervals of, say, every couple of months. Heti explained that writers get stuck in indecision; that there aren't really any right or wrong decisions. The important aspect is to make the decision, to choose. Even to choose arbitrarily is better than not to choose at all. To make your own fortune.

*

Our trip to Japan is part of a forty-six-day trip around the world. Six countries. Three continents. Two adults: Dan and I. Ten flights and three kids: ages three, six-turning-seven on the trip, and eight. In the late months of 2019, we fly high over the CN Tower, leaving Toronto's Pearson Airport, and land in San Francisco, California, then on to Hawaii, Japan, Thailand, a brief sojourn in Frankfurt, then on to Portugal and back home.

*

In Hiroshima, we lighten our load and leave our suitcases and any extra belongings in two train station lockers. We proceed to Kyoto with only two backpacks, carrying our necessities for a few nights. We fail to realize Ariel's sweatshirt is missing until we are in Kyoto, visiting Fushimi Inari: the shrine of the thousand torii gates. Our family of five is walking through the blood-orange sunrise arches, our location is remote, when Ariel complains of the cold air.

A light misting of rain descends on her bare arms from overcast skies. Goosebumps, tiny muscles contracting in unison, pinprick the length of her arms, spreading across her skin like wildfire.

She comes to a standstill in the middle of the trail, arms crossed, resolute. "I'm not going *anywhere*!"

Throngs of people pass by her, like a boulder in a waterfall. Our troupe pulls over, huddling to one side of the trail as much as we can to get out of the way.

"You're cold," I say. "Let's take a look in your backpack for your hoodie."

"It's not there." Ariel's scowling at me, as though I purpose-fully took the sweatshirt out of her bag and left it in the train sta-tion locker. Her anger riles my guilt and annoyance at myself and Dan — the adults — for not having double-checked that everyone had something warm to put on. She is eight, and at this point we are fairly exhausted from travel, time change, shifting diet, and culture shock.

I push through her backpack. No sweatshirt. *Shit, we must have left it in the locker.* But even as I think these words with hope, I remember Ariel wearing her sweatshirt on the train to Kyoto. Hundreds of bullet trains move through that station, on a pre-cise schedule, every day. Thousands upon thousands of people pass through. The sickening realization sinks in that not only does she not have her favourite sweatshirt now, when she is cold, but that she's left it on the train and she is never getting it back. Someone will surely take it.

I suck in my dignity as a parent and bribe her with candy. She takes what she can, then, arms crossed, exasperated and cold, stomps ahead of our family down the sacred path.

The sweatshirt is lost.

*

Three years before our trip, we lived in a beautiful home I dubbed "The Castle on the Hill" because it was built into a hillside, making the walk-in basement our principal entryway and giving the house a grandiose appearance. But we were house poor. We couldn't afford any travel while paying into that mortgage. We couldn't afford anything. And I longed to get away. I had a hard time getting my then baby and toddler outside to play in a tilted backyard without worrying about them barrel-rolling into the brick wall of the house. One side of the property had a finished wood deck with a scenic built-in koi pond. The pond was a drowning trap for mobile babies and toddlers and meant that I couldn't leave them outside alone — say, if I wanted to use the bathroom, or grab someone a snack — for even a few seconds. Dan frequently travelled for work, and I found myself trapped inside with two young kids, left behind, wanting to break free.

I approached Dan after work one day. "I have a *big idea*."

He nodded his head and held up one finger. "Hold on a minute." He poured himself a whisky. "Okay, let's hear it."

"What if," I proposed, my voice rising, "we sell our home and travel the world?"

The eagerness in my eyes must have said all he needed to know in that moment.

He paused a few seconds before answering.

"Okay," he said.

"Okay! Yes!"

"But would we bring the kids?"

"Of course!"

"Okay, good."

I was in the early stages of pregnancy with our third baby. The trip would ultimately take years to plan, but at the time, I envisioned us leaving when Penelope (who was yet to be born) was around eighteen months old.

We sold our home, and I slowly packed boxes during my pregnancy. I gave birth to Penelope in my bedroom, on the bed Dan and I shared, in The Castle on the Hill. When she was a few days old, friends and family gathered among the packed boxes to come meet our third-born, her milky scent tucked into the folds of her neck. When Penelope was just two weeks old, we moved into a more economical home that would allow us to afford our trip.

Dan and I had originally planned to go on a cruise where we could leave our luggage behind on the ship, enjoy meals provided, and we'd find ourselves in a new country every few days. But the cruises were outrageously expensive, booked up years in advance, and the right one wasn't popping up, even with a cruise representative helping us. As the planning year-mark ticked by, deep down I had a creeping suspicion that a cruise wasn't going to deliver the authentic types of experiences I imagined would both enlighten and pull us together as a family.

A year and a half into the process, the cruise saleswoman who had been helping us, a mother in her forties, died unexpectedly of brain cancer. One day I spoke to her on the phone about world cruise options, and a month later she was dead. Her sudden disappearance from this earth was a jolt to my system. Stunned from the shock and loss of her death, I realized time was slipping by. The solution came while watching the Disney movie *Tangled* with my daughters.

In *Tangled*, every year on her birthday, Rapunzel's parents, the King and Queen, release a flock of lit paper lanterns that cover the sky in glowing lights. Her parents perform this ritual yearly after Rapunzel is stolen from them, in the hopes she will see the lanterns and one day return home. Ariel loved the movie *Tangled*, though the witch character, Gothel, scared her. We must have watched *Tangled* a thousand times.

Was I researching Thailand? Did someone post an article online? I can't remember how I found out, but what I do remember is that once I learned the floating lanterns in *Tangled* were based on the real lantern festival of Loy Krathong in Chiang Mai, Thailand, I knew that my family had to go. The floating lanterns were the exact kind of authentic experience my kids could connect to and would be excited about — that I was excited about. The festival of Loy Krathong, which takes place yearly in the fall, became the starting point of our trip. I would work backward and around to get us there.

But the real reason for the trip? The real *real* reason.

I didn't want having a child with Down syndrome to hold our family back, to hold my husband and I back. To hold me back. Before she was even born, I was getting messages that our lives as parents to a child with Down syndrome would somehow be "less." Less desirable. Less status. Less time. Less perfect. I rightfully balked at the stereotypes of what a family "should" be. I could not accept that our lives should somehow be "less," that raising this child was going to be harder even if it was and would be. With dichotomous black-and-white thinking, I left no room for "less" to somehow mean "more." And harder for who, specifically? Typically mothers. Mothers who are expected to do the majority of the caring. I didn't want motherhood to be any harder than it already was.

But the truth goes deeper than that. In many cultures, having a child with Down syndrome is viewed as a bad omen, an ill fortune. While attending the 2014 World Down Syndrome Congress in Chennai, India, four years before our family trip, I met a woman from Ghana. She explained that her community, the friends and family from her village, viewed her son with Down syndrome as an ill omen, a punishment from the gods. After she gave birth to her son outside of the village, her homecoming was forbidden. I understood that some version of this belief had a hold in my own Western culture. Why else are babies with Down syndrome aborted at a staggering rate of 80 to 90 percent,[1] if not to suggest that our society views having a disabled child as a "bad thing"?

It is also true that I struggle with overly caring about what others think. And people, friends and family, doubted that we could pull off such a trip. I wanted to prove them wrong. The worst, I imagined, were the folks who believed that my daughter *shouldn't* travel. I knew people existed who didn't believe a child with Down syndrome was deserving of rich experiences. *What would she even get out of it, anyway?*, they might say, or *What a waste of money.* I wanted to shove every last Hawaiian sunset, every exploding firework and floating lantern, every ocean swim and elephant encounter and moment of awe from our trip in their faces. My daughter was as deserving as any child. I knew this in my heart. But who was I trying to convince by going on this trip? *Them* — or myself?

> *Am I ableist? Yes.*
> *Will I continue to learn more about ableism? Yes.*
> *Are most people ableist? No.*
> *Do most people care about individuals with Down syndrome? Yes.*
> *Is it okay to write a book about my daughter? No.*
> *Is it okay to write about my feelings toward my daughter? Yes.*
> *Will others understand her? No.*
> *Do I understand her? Yes.*
> *Does she understand herself? Yes.*
> *Is it important to have a happy life? Yes.*

✳

On our way to Departures at the Honolulu airport, Dan drives our rental car along the freeway as I look forlornly out the window. Japan, here we come. In the background, Israel Kamakawiwo'ole's

"Over the Rainbow" and strumming ukulele blares through the car speakers. A tear escapes and rolls down my cheek. I'm replaying the events of the past eight days in my mind. The wide-open turquoise sky and sunsets that fill eternity. The swell of the ocean and its inhabitants: black sea cucumbers and spiky sea urchins in my children's cupped hands; swimming in the sheltered tide pools; the giant sea turtles, our constant companions, present as we brave surfing the waves. The shaved ice, açai bowls, pineapple fields, and the fresh macadamia nuts packed somewhere in my bag. The scent of coconut will stay with me long after we're gone. Hawaii is my favourite stop. Hawaii is my favourite stop even though the unruly, untamed, unpredictable wilderness scares the hell out of me.

The first beach we go to, I run into the ocean waves, a welcome reprieve from the hot sand burning my feet, and I am immediately sucked under by the riptide, my hat ripped from my head, hair flopped over my face. Momentarily, I cannot breathe. In that moment, my realization is this: *I am the strongest swimmer in our family.* I come up sputtering salt water and forcing my feet into the sand, grasping for the shore, as the tepid water fights to pull me back in, my arms waving frantically, me screaming over the roar of the fierce wind to a husband who's carelessly spraying on sunscreen and attaching floaties to kids who cannot swim and are now careening toward me and will surely drown under the force of that pull. I will love Hawaii even as their small bodies advance, move toward me, toward the danger and the ocean that does not relent or care. I catch two of them in my arms, drop to my knees, my whole body thrumming from the threat. Ariel will read the fear in my face then, but three-year-old Penelope thinks Mommy is being funny, and she giggles at the dishevelled sight of me. Elyse, thankfully, is standing with her dad who, sun spray in hand, is oblivious to my inner turmoil. He takes me in, puzzled.

I will heed this warning, keep them safe. This time, under the blazing heat and waves that will snuff your breath out like a candle, fortune is on my side.

✦

In Sheila Heti's fictional work *Motherhood*,[2] the narrator asks the big question of whether she should become a mother. At the beginning of the book, readers are told the narrator has devised her own system of seeking answers using three coins. She asks a "yes" or "no" question, then throws three coins: if two or three heads turn up, the divine universe has responded with "yes"; two or three tails, "no." Three coins can similarly be used to read the *I Ching*, a book of ancient Chinese wisdom, and it is from this that Heti borrows and bases her system.

✦

Japan. Tokyo. We arrive. People, everywhere. Progress, concrete. The world tilts. We check into a hotel, squeeze our giant North American selves and meagre belongings into the tiny elevator (that's a lie: we had to take two trips to get everyone and our baggage up to our floor), collapse into sleep, then get up the next morning to explore this Eastern world. With some cajoling, we convince a cab driver to take the five of us to Senso-ji, a huge red and gold Buddhist temple in the centre of the city. Japanese taxis have a max capacity of four people. A special taxi is required to transport five. After our visit to the temple, I will ride with the three girls by myself, while Dan is forced to take a separate taxi back. When I planned our itinerary, did I know that Senso-ji had O-mikuji, hand-held fortunes? I can no longer be sure, but what I do know is that when we move through the crowds, I see dark-haired citizens holding rectangular pieces of paper in their hands. And I want one.

Before we've even stepped through the gates to find our fortunes, trouble is brewing. The kids are wrangy from hunger, and while I insist we ask someone to photograph our family in the ornate entryway, Dan is exasperated by the kids' wails and escape tactics and my nonchalance. He grabs the phone from my hand and in a show of poor sportsmanship takes the picture of his belligerent family himself. A passerby then insists he get in the photo, which pleases me, but only further irritates the already impatient.

During our travels in Asia, everyday folk have greeted three-year-old Penelope with adoration and wonder. Not-so-discreet amateur photographers approach to take pictures of her lush curls, an apparent rarity and curiosity that draws intent stares. Dan and I have been intrigued that it is Penelope's curls that stand out — not our daughter with Down syndrome. The Asians-photographing-our-child phenomenon is absurd and hilarious to our sleep-deprived minds, and we have made a game out of counter-photographing the image-takers.

Having made it only inside the archway gate of the shrine we've come to see, with Elyse refusing to walk and slouched down in the umbrella stroller and Penelope running around wildly, scowling at her admirers, we retreat outside the gates to a 7-Eleven, and the girls famously eat spaghetti in Japan, while Dan and I eat poor-man's bento boxes, sitting on the storefront curb. Once fortified, we make our way back through the gates and inside Senso-ji toward the temple, to find our fortunes.

✳

Sheila Heti chose coin flipping. Another form of random fortune-telling is the O-mikuji, a popular activity at temples and shrines in Japan. To find your fortune, you draw a chopstick-like baton out of the hole in the box. The stick bears a number. The number corresponds to a symbol on a large chest of small drawers. Inside the drawers are fortunes.

I recall my fortune and Dan's fortune the most clearly because they broke the tension of our travels, adding levity and humour, the essential ingredient to spending any extended amount of time with another adult and in the presence of small children, in wacky time zones. Based on our two fortunes, I can piece together the rest — who else in our family got what. Penelope's fortune was good: "Washing off all bad things in the past, now everything is clear and clean." Ariel drew first and pulled "Bad Fortune," and then immediately wanted to try again, causing a fight over the box of "chopsticks" with Penelope. Dan, whose bad mood permeated the air like a low-hanging cloud from chasing Elyse around while I helped sort out Ariel and Penelope, drew last and also received "Bad Fortune," which, we both mused, befitted his mood.

No. 69, "Bad Fortune":

> The clear moon is covered by thick clouds. The sky got dark and doesn't get fine. The red flower decayed to a half, the bad fortune is found among the happiness … Your request will not be granted. Don't get relaxed to care the patient. The lost article will not be found. The person you wait for will not appear. Building a new house and removal are both no good. It is no good to start a trip. Marriage, of any kind and new employment are all bad.

On the plus side, pulling bad luck brought comic relief to the non-believer. We wondered what it meant to receive the advice not to travel while travelling, and that marriage is bad while married. Elyse, who initially refused to participate in O-mikuji by running away, was eventually caught, thanks to grumpy Dan, and I know this because I insisted Dan take a picture to capture the moment. I helped her draw her fortune from the box. Elyse's fortune was also good, like Penelope's, but with a caveat: "Good Fortune *in Future*":

> There are various kinds of stones but you still can't distinguish jewels from stones. If you want to succeed in life. You'll come across lots of difficulties and become sad. What you hope will be completed just like flowers bloom on old branches … Your wishes will be realized in the end.

As is customary, we tied the two bad fortunes to a wire alongside a slew of other ill fortunes, the idea being to leave the bad fortune behind in the hopes of shaking it off.

> *Where else should we travel as a family? Should we*
> *travel within Canada? No.*
> *Europe? Yes.*
> *The U.S.? Yes.*
> *Other countries? No.*
> *Other continents? No.*

*

That night, fortunes in hand, we stay at a traditional Japanese inn, a ryokan, in Kyoto, then return to the train station the next morning to continue on our journey to Hiroshima. I ask the attendant at the ticket booth if, by chance, they have a lost and found. We have to backtrack anyway to the larger station we arrived at only the day before — no harm in asking.

"What train were you on?" the attendant asks me, quite serious-ly. *Give me the exact time.*

Dan and I figure there have been hundreds of trains in the past day, coming and going. We assume Ariel's sweatshirt is gone, never to be seen again.

But there is a ticket, a lost-and-found item, being held at the police station in Hiroshima from that exact train: a child's pink sweatshirt.

✦

Am I here to write? Yes.
Should I write about my children? Yes.
Should I write about travelling? Yes.
Should I write about the value of a life? Yes.
Should I write about Down syndrome? No.
Should I write about birds? Yes.
Will I have a lucky fortune? No.
Will Dan? No.
Ariel? No.
Elyse? Yes.
Penelope? Yes.
Is it important to stop and listen to the birds sing?
Yes.

✦

By the time we arrive in Chiang Mai, Thailand, to see the lantern festival, we have already been travelling for twenty-five days. In the pool at our riverside hotel, Elyse befriends a little French boy with long, dark lashes, after repeatedly splashing his mother, who good-naturedly splashes back. While Elyse understands French, she and the little boy speak in the universal language of children, with squirming bodies and gleeful facial expressions. Elyse swims next to the boy and cheers for him while he performs cannonball after cannonball off the pool edge.

Later, he finds me in the lobby on his way to dinner, his hair neatly coifed, wearing a crisp, clean, button-up gingham T-shirt. He unfurls a handful of wrapped candies palmed in his hand.

"*Mais, où est Elyse?*" He looks around for his new friend. He swam and played with all three of our girls, but the candies are for Elyse.

I apologize, "*Elle est dans sa chambre.*"

His drooping, disappointed face is heartwarming, to say the least. I promise we'll catch up with him later — though I'm not sure we ever did.

That night, with some trepidation, I sign our family up to board the hotel's mini cruise into the heart of town, where we will experience the lantern festival. By this point in our trip, Elyse has already been pushed to the edge of her limits. Hiking through the jungle in a blanket of heat, feeding elephants without enclosures, then moving swiftly out of their way when they reverse. Paddling into the Pacific alongside sea turtles, tandem surfing and crashing through a wave that nearly capsizes her and her experienced co-rider, the surf-shop owner. "That was close," the surf owner goddess says to me afterward, of her experience guiding Elyse, once they are safely back on the beach. The dangers on our trip have been as real as Elyse's fears and discomfort. Novel situations are off-putting to her as it is. She wailed for the entire duration of our diesel-fuelled taxi-boat ride in Bangkok, her screams barely audible over the roar of the exposed engine. Helplessly, we covered her ears and held her close. Why will this river cruise be any different?

That evening of the festival will be particularly challenging for Elyse for several reasons: the late night, the bright sights, the loud and unexpected sounds, the turbulence of the boat moving through the water, and the novelty of the situation each spell potential disaster. I cringe at the thought of the stress I will be putting Elyse through. But when weighing the pros and cons, I decide the experience of thousands of floating lanterns in the water and sky will be worth it.

Is this madness, these excursions that expose my children to adventure and danger? Am I a "crazy" mom, to want this for my family and for myself? Crazy in the sense Marguerite Duras meant when she said, "I believe that always, or almost always, in all child hoods and in all the lives that follow them, the mother represents madness. Our mothers always remain the strangest, craziest people we've ever met."[3]

The word "crazy" is problematic from a mental health stigma standpoint, but I would rather be called "crazy" than "boring and lifeless." I would rather know I have pushed myself and those I love to live fully in the best way I know how. Conversely, I see madness in a "resignation-to-life" mindset. I see madness in inertia.

I have not backed down from pushing Elyse into her fears, and neither has she backed down from her protests, and often we meet in the middle.

To mitigate the overwhelming sensory experience, Dan and I reluctantly bring earphones and an iPad on the boat with us. While I could have allowed myself to feel ashamed about this parenting move, instead I feel relief. After she shows signs of distress, we give Elyse the device and she is then able to experience the festival at her own level. And our fellow companions, in that intimate space, are spared her tears.

Our boat reaches its destination in old-town Chiang Mai, and we are thoroughly enchanted by the experience of thousands of glowing lights rising in unison. At the height of the beauty and chaos, Elyse chooses to take off her earphones and comes to join me as I crouch, putting her little hand on my shoulder. Together, we release a krathong, a candle-lit banana-shaped boat, into the water on behalf of our family. It is a beautiful moment, and if I insisted Elyse do things solely my way, it would never have happened.

✦

The O-mikuji fortune I drew was No. 96, "The Best Fortune":

> Relying upon a person in higher rank for help to succeed in one's life is just like a cock tries to fly following a phoenix and perches on a higher twig. Poling a boat across the stream is a simile of your getting along well with others in this world.
>
> You will rise in the world and be wealthy.
>
> Your wish will come true, so you should be modest for everything. The sick person will get well. The lost article will be found. The person you are waiting for will come. Building a new house and removal are both good. It is good to make a travel. Both marriage and employment are good.

✦

Canada to California, Cali to Hawaii, Hawaii to Japan to Thailand to Frankfurt to Portugal. Home. Dan's favourite stop on our around-the-world trip was Japan. In Japan, everything fell in its right place. Crime seemed non-existent. Litter was nowhere to be found. Public washrooms were clean and pleasant. Vending machines sold hot pizza. Lost sweatshirts were turned in.

We picked up Ariel's favourite sweatshirt at the lost and found at the police station in Hiroshima. Ariel slid her arms back inside its warmth, grateful. *The lost article is found.*

> *Does getting the luckiest fortune mean anything?*
> *Yes.*
> *Does getting the best fortune mean I will have the best life? Yes.*

❦

On Koh Samui, an island off the east coast of Thailand, I am seeking peace from our travels. I didn't know it at the time, but I was, and I was frantic to find it.

I finally settle down into a chair poolside, facing the ocean, and crack open my book, *Natalie Tan's Book of Luck and Fortune*, by Roselle Lim, and I come across the line, "My mother had once compared compliments to birds; if you don't chase after them, they come on their own."[4] Penelope takes off behind the bush and makes a mad dash, barefoot, back in the direction of our villa, where a fluorescent green snake is hanging from our thatched roof. I chase her, catch her, but it's one thing after another. I haven't had a moment's peace. Dan dutifully gets up and offers to accompany our two restless girls back to our villa. I stay behind with Elyse, who can be quite restless herself.

Wordlessly, I welcome Elyse into the lounge chair beside mine, into my shroud of reading. She opens her Berenstain Bears book, and — looking quite philosophical and bookwormish — my then seven-year-old dives into her text as I dive into mine.

Meanwhile, two birds perch nearby, as though waiting for their cue to enter, and begin singing a lovely, melodic call. The beck and call, back and forth, is like a prayer ringing out, then answered.

The smaller of the two departs and just the one bird, with its bright orange beak and yellow-winged stripe against black feathers, is left delivering its magnificent tune. Its song is striking and pierces the empty air, filling the space with the sound of its joy.

Elyse pauses her reading to enjoy the song too, as I note her gaze tilt up from the page. I am surprised to see we are both looking at the same bird.

You can't seek out songs of joy and peace; peace is a state of mind to be embodied, not necessarily a physical space. When a song is yours to hear, your ears will be open to hearing it. The tune will carry to you. Some songs you can hear only when your ears are open to listening. This is the moment I will recall vividly after our trip, that I will come back to in my mind and turn over and over, like a coin, in surrender: The sun blanching out the sky in its ferocity, hanging low and heavy, the melodic sound of waves returning to shore. The still air and the crisp call of the bird crying out. Elyse, in the chair beside mine, both of us reading and then attuned to the bird. What more could be asked of this life? What turn of fortune could be sweeter? And in that moment, looking back, I see my own ableism understood anew: *we were both looking at the same bird.* However my daughter experienced the sensation of that bird's song wasn't for me or anyone else to judge, and the same could be said for my own interpretation. We were both present to witness the miracle of life. Reclined in the sun beside me, my daughter didn't miss anything — and neither did I.

Acknowledgements

INTERCONNECTEDNESS IS AT the heart of this book. Writing these narratives has filled my life for the past three — but really eleven — years. I've met incredible people in the Down syndrome and literary communities, and as a teacher and parent, and everyone I've interacted with has shaped me and this book in some way. Thank you for these connections, and to you, dear reader, for finding these pages.

Thank you to family for your love and support: Mom and Dad, Jim and Helga Purdham, Brad and Stace, Alexis and Sean, Mark and Medrie Purdham (brilliant poet, prof, and mentor), nieces and nephews: Kianna, Sophie, Hudson, Auston, Julian, Aiden, Isla, Tilly, Rowan, Victor. Grandma Marie and the Hunt family. The McFarlane clan. Lindsey, yogi and retreat partner extraordinaire. The Freilers. The Purdhams across the pond. You are loved.

To my high school friends, whose friendship shines bright decades later: Ames, Ash, Jods, Kareen, Katers, Megs, Mel, and Trace.

To teacher colleagues, book club friends, writing and editing students, and The Write Retreat participants, past and present; from Western, to the Peel District School Board, to Trent University main campus, Durham and beyond: thank you for your support and for inspiring me.

To the Down syndrome and disability community, especially fellow parents and various Down syndrome associations — local (Down Syndrome Association of Hamilton, Halton Down Syndrome Association, Down Syndrome Association of Toronto), regional (Down Syndrome Association of Ontario), national (Canadian Down Syndrome Society, Down Syndrome Resource Foundation), and international (Down Syndrome International) — for the immeasurable support and education I've received through you in various ways. To Emily Boycott: fellow gymnast, speaking partner, book lover, and Special Olympian — this book is also for you.

To the University of King's College MFA Community, especially Kim Pittaway, Dean, and Stephen, and the pandemic cohort(s). With special thanks to my incredible mentors who helped shape many of the essays in this collection: Jane Silcott, Ayelet Tsabari, and Cooper Lee Bombardier. To the other members of the King's Six: Martha, Maryanne, Jess, Chris, and Kate, who helped get me through the first year; and to Jason Schreurs's writing-group members for weekly meet-ups that sustained me. To Taslim, fellow teacher; Kirsten, fellow paddler; Tammy, fellow travel partner. This writing community continues to enrich my life and work.

My thanks to Martha for weekly check-ins, farm retreats, and her careful eye and unwavering encouragement and support.

Thank you to the Humber School for Writers, where I began this work in a different form, and to mentor M.G. Vassanji, who taught me how to get started: "Just write."

Thank you to the Sage Hill Writing community and especially to the brilliant 2023 Online Summer Course cohort, who provided feedback on these essays: Micheline, Kathleen, Alison, Patti, and Kelly. A big thank you to mentor Lorri Neilsen Glenn for her lessons and encouragement to get my manuscript out at just the right time.

To the many writers who have supported my work in some way: Kim Fahner, Dr. Catherine McKercher, Alison Wearing, Hollay Ghadery, Laura Rock Gaughan, Natalie Harrison, Larry Hendel, Alicia Elliott, Sheila Heti, Lindsay Wong, Amanda Leduc, Susan Olding, Gillian Turnbull, Jen Sookfong Lee, Stacey May Fowles, Leslie Means, Leanne Milech, Eufemia Fantetti, Jessica Westhead, Lindsay Zier-Vogel, Lisa Browning, Liisa Kovala, Alison Fishburn, Glen Hoos, Sean Carroll, Ziya Tong, Scott Colby, Howard Elliott, JP Fozo, Betsy Warland, Jack Wang, and innumerable others whose books have left their indelible mark.

To Dundurn Press, my sincerest thanks and gratitude goes to the entire team, especially: Meghan Macdonald, Erin Pinksen, Rajdeep Singh, Laura Boyle, and Vicky Bell. Special thank you to my editor, Megan Beadle: instant happy tears on the island of Naxos because you made me feel seen. Thank you for championing my work and for showcasing a story written by a mother to a child with Down syndrome (one of the first of its kind in Canadian creative nonfiction literature).

To Ariel, you made me a mother. Thank you for our Greece adventures and for your fierce lion heart. I love you.

To Penelope, my animal whisperer with the old-poet's soul. Thanks for the nightly stories, both the ones we write and the ones we read. I love you.

To Elyse, my star. Thank you for your humour, for reminding me to slow down and be in the moment, and for widening my view of the world. I love you.

To Dan, my life partner. You are my string and I am your balloon. You keep me grounded and I give you reason to look up at the sky. It's a bigger, better world with you in it. Thank you for being my first reader, believing in me most, and for giving of yourself so that I could write and become the best version of myself. Meet you at the warm spot. I love you more.

The author wishes to acknowledge the generous financial support of Access Copyright Foundation. She was awarded a Professional Development Grant to attend Sage Hill Writing, where she worked on this manuscript (Online, Summer Program 2023).

A shortened version of "The Mushroom" appeared in the anthology *So God Made A Mother*, edited by Leslie Means (Tyndale Momentum, 2023).

"The Giving Tree" appeared in the anthology *Good Mom on Paper*, edited by Stacey May Fowles and Jen Sookfong Lee (Book*hug Press, 2022).

"Untethered" appeared in the anthology *Animals and Our Emotional Wellbeing*, edited by Lisa Browning (One Thousand Trees, 2021).

Notes

THREE, TWO, ONE

1   Len Leshin, "Medical Concerns in Babies with Down Syndrome," in *Babies with Down Syndrome: A New Parents' Guide, 3rd ed.*, ed. Susan J. Skallerup (Bethesda: Woodbine House, 2008), 75–102.

2   "World Down Syndrome Day," Down Syndrome International, accessed January 21, 2024, worlddownsyndromeday.org.

ELEVEN YEARS A COUNTRY

1   Wendell Berry, "The Country of Marriage," in *The Country of Marriage* (Berkeley: Counterpoint, 2013), 4–7.

2   Berry, "The Country of Marriage," 4–7.

THE GOLDEN HOUR

1   Ray Bradbury, "All Summer in a Day," *Magazine of Fantasy & Science Fiction 6*, March 1954, no. 3: 8–12.

I DON'T DO DISABILITY

1   Audre Lorde, *Sister Outsider: Essays and Speeches* (Berkeley: Crossing Press, 2007).

2   Margaret Atwood, "Princess Clothing," in *Dearly: Poems* (Toronto: McClelland & Stewart, 2020), 21.

3   Atwood, "Princess Clothing," 21.

4   Chahira Kozma, "What Is Down Syndrome?," in *Babies with Down Syndrome: A New Parents' Guide, 3rd ed.*, ed. Susan J. Skallerup (Bethesda: Woodbine House, 2008), 1–43.

5   Judith L. Fridovich-Keil, "Human Genome," *Encyclopedia Britannica*, accessed January 21, 2024, britannica.com/science/human-genome.

6   Université de Genève, "The Down Syndrome 'Super Genome.'" *ScienceDaily*, accessed January 19, 2018, sciencedaily.com/releases/2018/01/180119090148.htm.

7   Université de Genève, "The Down Syndrome 'Super Genome.'"

8   Dan Purdham, "Superbaby," adellepurdham.ca/superbaby-by-dan-purdham/.

9   Université de Genève, "The Down Syndrome 'Super Genome.'"

10   Université de Genève, "The Down Syndrome 'Super Genome.'"

11   "Chance of Chromosomal Difference Based on Age," *Prenatal Screening Ontario*, accessed January 21, 2024, prenatalscreeningontario.ca/en/pso/prenatal-screening-options/chance-of-chromosome-differences-based-on-age.aspx.

12   Kozma, "What Is Down Syndrome?," 1–43.

13   Kozma, "What Is Down Syndrome?,"1–43.

14   Beautiful News South Africa, "Shéri Defied the Down Syndrome Odds to Carve Her Own Place in History," IOL, accessed January 21, 2024, iol.co.za/travel/south-africa/free-state/Shéri-defied-the-down-syndrome-odds-to-carve-her-own-place-in-history-17487284.

15   Ryan Porter, "Amanda Leduc's Disability Justice Critique of Fairy Tales Speaks to Our Own Ableist Society," *Quill & Quire*, January 2020, quillandquire.com/authors/amanda-leducs-disability-justice-critique-of-fairy-tales-speaks-to-our-own-ableist-society/.

EVERYDAY DEVOTION

1   "End," *Oxford Learner's Dictionary*, accessed January 21, 2024, oxfordlearnersdictionaries.com/definition/english/end_1?q=end.

2 "Beginning," *Oxford Learner's Dictionary*, accessed January 21, 2024, oxfordlearnersdictionaries.com/definition/english /beginning?q=beginning.

3 Chloe Caldwell, *I'll Tell You in Person* (Minneapolis: Coffee House Press, 2016), 95.

4 Mary Oliver, *Upstream: Selected Essays* (New York: Penguin Press, 2016), 8.

A LOON

1 Sy Montgomery, "Loon," *Encyclopedia Britannica*, accessed January 21, 2024, britannica.com/animal/loon-bird.

2 Valerie Assinewe, "How Much Do You Know About the Common Loon?," *Nature Canada*, last modified September 1, 2015, naturecanada.ca/news/blog/how-much-do-you-know-about-the -common-loon/.

3 Montgomery, "Loon."

4 Valerie Assinewe, "The Common Loon: What Are They Saying?," *Nature Canada*, last modified September 17, 2015, naturecanada .ca/news/blog/the-common-loon-what-are-they-saying/.

HOW TO MAKE NEW LOVE

1 National Geographic Society, "The Rock Cycle," *National Geographic Education*, last modified December 13, 2023, education .nationalgeographic.org/resource/rock-cycle/.

2 Mandy Len Catron, *How to Fall in Love with Anyone: A Memoir in Essays* (New York: Simon & Schuster, 2017).

3 Mandy Len Catron, "To Fall in Love with Anyone, Do This," *New York Times*, January 9, 2015, nytimes.com/2015/01/11/style/ modern-love-to-fall-in-love-with-anyone-do-this.html.

4 Daniel Jones, "The 36 Questions That Lead to Love," *New York Times*, January 9, 2015, nytimes.com/2015/01/09/style/no-37-big -wedding-or-small.html.

5 Jones, "The 36 Questions."

6 National Geographic Society, "The Rock Cycle."

7 Jones, "The 36 Questions."

8   National Geographic Society, "The Rock Cycle."
9   Jones, "The 36 Questions."

THE MUSHROOM
1   Peter Wohlleben, *The Hidden Life of Trees: The Illustrated Edition* (Vancouver: Greystone Books, 2015).
2   Wohlleben, *The Hidden Life of Trees.*
3   *Fantastic Fungi*, directed by Louie Schwartzberg (Los Angeles: Moving Art, 2019).
4   Wohlleben, *The Hidden Life of Trees.*
5   Kim Fahner, "Pole Star," in *These Wings* (St. John's: Pedlar Press, 2019), 31.
6   *Fantastic Fungi.*
7   *Fantastic Fungi.*
8   *Fantastic Fungi.*

THE GIVING TREE
1   Richard Powers, *The Overstory* (New York: W.W. Norton & Company, 2018), 221.
2   Shel Silverstein, *The Giving Tree* (New York: Harper Collins, 1964).
3   Silverstein, 22–24.
4   Silverstein, 43–46.
5   Haruki Murakami, *What I Talk About When I Talk About Running: A Memoir* (Toronto: Anchor Canada, 2009), 50.
6   Eren Orbey, "A Mother's Steely Portraits of Her Daughter's Life with Down Syndrome," *New Yorker*, August 18, 2020, newyorker.com /culture/photo-booth/a-mothers-steely-portraits-of-her-daughters -life-with-down-syndrome.
7   Powers, *The Overstory*, 221.
8   Powers, *The Overstory*, 222.

REVERBERATIONS OF INSTITUTIONAL VIOLENCE: A SPECTRUM
1   Catherine McKercher, *Shut Away: When Down Syndrome was a Life Sentence* (Fredricton: Goose Lane, 2019).
2   McKercher, *Shut Away*, 215.

3 McKercher, *Shut Away*, 215.
4 McKercher, *Shut Away*, 215.
5 McKercher, *Shut Away*, 215.
6 McKercher, *Shut Away*, 204–5.

A RECLAMATION

1 Jennifer Baggett, Holly C. Corbett, and Amanda Pressner, *The Lost Girls: Three Friends. Four Continents. One Unconventional Detour Around the World* (New York: Harper Collins, 2010).
2 McKercher, *Shut Away*, 215.
3 McKercher, *Shut Away*, 215.
4 "About Down Syndrome," National Down Syndrome Society, accessed January 21, 2024, ndss.org/about#p_68.
5 "About Down Syndrome."

UNTETHERED

1 Eula Biss, *On Immunity: An Inoculation* (Minneapolis: Graywolf Press, 2015).

WILD HORSES

1 Donna Haraway, *Simians, Cyborgs and Women: The Reinvention of Nature* (New York: Routledge, 1991), 224.
2 Ananya Mandal, "What Is Ginseng?," *News Medical Life Sciences*, last modified June 14, 2023, news-medical.net/health/What-is -Ginseng.aspx
3 Arlene Semeco, "7 Proven Health Benefits of Ginseng," *Healthline*, last modified December 15, 2023, healthline.com/nutrition /ginseng-benefits.

A THIN LINE

1 Zia Tong, *The Reality Bubble: Blind Spots, Hidden Truths, and the Dangerous Illusions that Shape Our World* (Toronto: Penguin Random House, 2019), 99.
2 Tong, *The Reality Bubble*, 57.
3 Tong, *The Reality Bubble*, 58.

4   "The Cosmic Distance Scale," NASA, last modified October 22, 2020, imagine.gsfc.nasa.gov/features/cosmic/milkyway_info.html.

5   Tong, *The Reality Bubble*, 57.

6   Tong, *The Reality Bubble*, 59.

7   Robert Munsch and Michael Martchenko (Illustrator), *The Paperbag Princess* (Toronto: Annick Press, 1980), 19.

8   Lorde, *Sister Outsider*, 31.

9   Tong, *The Reality Bubble*, 68.

10 Matthew Barker, "Peterborough Family Remembers Cassy: 'She Was So Loved,'" *Peterborough Examiner*, September 27, 2021, thepeteroroughexaminer.com/news/peterborough-region /peterborough-family-remembers-cassy-she-was-so-loved/article _01dfe0a0-c37f-54b1-bd77-c4c14b880cc8.html.

CEPHEID: AN ASTRONOMY OF FEMALE FRIENDSHIP

1   "Cepheids," NASA, accessed January 22, 2024, starchild.gsfc.nasa .gov/docs/StarChild/questions/cepheids.html#.

2   Barbara Ryden, "The Cosmic Distance Scale," Ohio State University, February 25, 2003, astronomy.ohio-state.edu/ryden.1 /ast162_8/notes33.html#.

3   "Cepheid Variables as Cosmic Yardsticks," NASA, last modified October 22, 2020, imagine.gsfc.nasa.gov/science/questions/cepheid .html#.

4   "Cepheid Variable Stars RS Puppis," NASA, accessed January 22, 2024, smd-cms.nasa.gov/wp-content/uploads/2023/07/hubble-litho -cepheid-rs-puppis.pdf.

5   "Cepheid Variables as Cosmic Yardsticks."

6   "Cepheid Variables as Cosmic Yardsticks."

APORIA

1   Annie Dillard, "Seeing," in *The Abundance: Narrative Essays Old and New* (New York: ECCO, 2016), 172.

2   Bahar Orang, *Where Things Touch: A Meditation on Beauty* (Toronto: Book Hug Press, 2020), 7.

3   Elizabeth Barrett Browning, "How Do I Love Thee? (Sonnet 43)," Poets.org, accessed January 22, 2024, poets.org/poem/how -do-i-love-thee-sonnet-43.

4   Mary Oliver, "The Summer Day," in *House of Light* (Boston: Beacon Press, 1990).

THE BEST FORTUNE

1   Jaime L. Natoli, Deborah L. Ackerman, Suzanne McDermott, and Janice G. Edwards, "Prenatal Diagnosis of Down Syndrome: a Systematic Review of Termination Rates (1995–2011)," *Prenatal Diagnosis*, February 2012, no: 32,2: 142–53.

2   Sheila Heti, *Motherhood* (Toronto: Vintage Canada, 2018).

3   Marguerite Duras, *Practicalities* (New York: Grove Press, 1993).

4   Roselle Lim, *Natalie Tan's Book of Luck & Fortune* (New York: Berkley, 2019), 118.

About the Author

Adelle Purdham is a writer, teacher, and parent disability advocate. She holds an MFA in Creative Nonfiction from the University of King's College and is a qualified French teacher. She is also a graduate of the Humber College Creative Writing program. Her poetry and prose appear in literary journals, anthologies, magazines, newspapers, and online. Adelle's essays have been finalists in several literary contests, including The Writers' Union of Canada Short Prose Competition, *EVENT Magazine* and the *Fiddlehead*'s creative nonfiction contests. She is founder of The Write Retreat, facilitating workshops for women writers to create. Adelle is a sessional course instructor at Trent University-Durham, where she teaches creative writing. She lives and writes in her hometown, Nogojiwanong (Peterborough), Ontario.

www.ingramcontent.com/pod-product-compliance
Lightning Source LLC
Chambersburg PA
CBHW020530270326
41927CB00006B/520